Easy Meditation Lessons

William Bodri
Lee Shu-Mei

ISBN-13: 978-0615783611
ISBN-10: 0615783619

DEDICATION

To all the people who want very simple basic lessons on how to meditate. May these simple lessons help you get started at calming your mind, increasing your vitality and improving your health, lengthening your life-span, and may they also lead to the biggest benefit of them all, which is spiritual progress. We are all seeking peace and happiness, and it is through meditation that we can achieve higher mind and spirit. May you work hard enough to achieve all these results which are also the true objectives of the yoga and martial arts traditions.

CONTENTS

ACKNOWLEDGMENTS

When we first wrote *Twenty-Five Doors to Meditation*, the idea was to produce a simple how-to book on many different types of meditation you might practice. Each lesson soon became bigger than anticipated because we started to include all sorts of rare information not found in print, and so the size of the book exploded. Then came a second attempt to write a simple how-to book on meditation that became *The Little Book of Meditation*, and the size of this book exploded as well. Even though we cut down on the number of meditation methods revealed, once again we tried to include comprehensive details and other important information that caused the book to become larger. If you really want in-depth or more advanced information on how to meditate, this is the book to read. Finally, Keven Duff in Hong Kong asked us to try one more time to produce the simplest of books that has very basic meditation lessons without all the details that more advanced practitioners want to know. "Most of the people I talk to just want simple meditation instructions. They are frustrated with not making much progress and convinced they cannot meditate, so can you just make something simpler?" With two strikes against us in writing a small book, per Keven's request we finally set out once again to produce the simple book we always wanted. We have tried to reduce all the meditation lessons to the basics and where appropriate, reveal where these instructions match with the popular yoga and martial arts traditions. It goes without saying that without the instructions of our teacher, Nan Huai-Chin, we would not have undertaken the task of writing this book for you.

i

1
INTRODUCTION

After a few unsuccessful efforts, many people tell us that they have given up trying to learn meditation. They want to experience internal mental peace and quiet that is free of stress and anxiety, and so they have heard they should learn how to meditate. In trying to meditate, however, they sit down, close their eyes and then try to let go of all their thoughts as they have been instructed, but their mind still seems just as busy as before. Thoughts are still bouncing all around running from place to place, and they cannot find any of the mental peace they were promised.

Since this happens every time they close their eyes, they quickly give up on the effort of learning meditation. "It's just too difficult," they complain. They tell us they cannot calm down to touch the inner peace people others are achieving, and so they totally abandon the attempt.

"Where is all the internal peace and tranquility from

meditation that people are talking about?" they ask us. "I'm not feeling less stressful, relaxed or quiet inside at all. My mind is still so busy. In fact, now that I notice it, it seems even busier than before. I give up. I really cannot meditate. It must not work for me. It is just too difficult."

Because practitioners do not quickly experience any type of mental calming, therefore they think they cannot meditate at all or that meditation doesn't work for them. The actual truth is that they were usually practicing the wrong way, or they were practicing correctly and *expecting instant results* without giving themselves enough time to learn how to reach a state of internal serenity. It takes time to master any new skill so this rule certainly applies to meditation, too. Learning how to meditate and calm your mind requires just as much time as learning how to do anything new.

Just as you cannot expect instant results when you are learning how to ride a bike, you therefore cannot expect to be able to instantly calm your mind without going through a period of learning and practice effort. Don't be so hard on yourself in expecting instant results. You must cut yourself some slack and give yourself some time.

The goal of learning meditation is certainly worthwhile, for if you could already calm your mind and reach a state of instant peace then you wouldn't want to learn meditation in the first place. We all need more peace and less stress in our lives. We all need to learn how to relax, and meditation is the answer to the problem of mental busyness, so let's take the time to learn how to do it correctly, and then the fruits will grow.

Unfortunately, no one bothers to tell beginners that it takes time to learn how to rest the mind because you have established a habit of busying it all your life. Because no one tells practitioners they are trying to break old habits, which everyone knows takes time, people often give up trying to learn how to meditate before they really get started. They say "I can't meditate" or "It doesn't work for me" before they even give it a proper go. Some people even fall asleep when they start to practice, and because this happens they also feel they cannot learn meditation. Of course there is a remedy for this, but they often give up rather than use it because they just don't have any guidance.

People often have some expectations for what they want to happen because of meditation, and when they don't get those results quickly they feel frustrated. This is natural. They think they should just be able to sit down and instantly enter into a deep state of calm right away without having to go through any training period. Is that a realistic expectation?

Learning meditation is just like training a muscle, in this case the "mind muscle." Everyone knows, from prior experience, that training a muscle takes time and the persistence of repeated effort. If that's the case with training muscles, then learning how to meditate should also take some time and diligent effort as well. You are training yourself how to relax, and this requires that you break old habits that prevent you from doing this.

If you could instantly find the natural purity of your mind that is there beneath all your mental chatter then you wouldn't need to learn meditation in the first place. Therefore it is natural to expect that you must train yourself in some special way to be able to experience the internal purity of your natural mind, and that training effort is why the time spent in meditation is called "meditation *practice*." Once you've gotten the basics down, however, then it becomes easier and easier over time to reach deeper and deeper states of internal peace and quiet rather quickly. You will even learn how to carry those states of clarity and calm into your regular life, which is something we all want. Who doesn't want a mind that is quicker, more clear and free of distractions?

The reason that meditation becomes easier over time is because your body and its internal energy flows actually transform due to the repeated practice of meditation. What we call the acupuncture meridians, or internal energy (*chi*) channels of the body, begin to open due to meditation practice and after they have all become fully opened, your vital energy will flow much more freely. That more harmonious circulation of internal energy will lead to a more peaceful mind free of countless disturbances because your thoughts are connected to that energy flow.

There are many benefits to improving the flow of vital energy within your body. This allows you to enter into a peaceful mental state much more quickly, and also leads to positive health and longevity benefits as well. It certainly leads to more energy and vigor. Many cultures talk about the health and longevity benefits of meditation which they have often witnessed—such as your body becoming softer, more flexible, warmer and just plain healthier over time—and modern science is starting to prove all sorts of other positive physical benefits to meditation, too. Even the rough edges of a difficult personality may soften due to meditation practice.

The very hardest part in learning how to meditate is just getting started and then sticking with your meditation practice past that initial learning phase. Therefore you shouldn't immediately give up just because your mind still seems busy inside and you think you aren't making any progress. Sometimes people have made a lot of progress in just a short while, but they don't even realize it. This is because they lack the strong powers of introspection which would allow them to measure things clearly.

On the other hand, sometimes practitioners don't seem to experience progress because they haven't been meditating correctly. The biggest fault of meditation practice is that practitioners usually cling to their thoughts even though they are taught to just know them without becoming attached to them. You let them come and go without clinging to them. Sometimes practitioners also haven't given themselves enough time to produce noticeable progress, such as seeing their minds become clearer, and this lack of patience causes them to lose heart as well.

You should not be too hard on yourself in demanding instant results when you are first learning how to meditate. Everything worthwhile requires some time and effort to learn how to do it well, and learning meditation follows this principle, too. In this small book we will therefore introduce several different meditation methods you can try and will explain the proper way to practice each one as well as how it works. If you follow these easy step-by-step instructions, you will be meditating correctly and experiencing all its great benefits in the shortest period possible.

Some people practice meditation solely for health results. Some practice so that they can have more energy and vigor. Some practice meditation because they say it helps them be more clear and creative, or because it helps them improve their ability to concentrate for long periods of time. Because it teaches you how to ignore mental distractions, meditation is one of the best ways to learn concentration.

Some people practice meditation on a daily basis so that they will live longer with less health issues (because they attain a higher quality of life). Some practice so they can handle stress better, and so that they can learn how to quickly relax by quieting their mind. Some people even practice meditation for spiritual purposes. If you are one of those people who has an intense desire for spirit and wisdom, it sits near you waiting to be retrieved through meditation practice. It is the way to higher mind and spirit.

No matter what your ultimate objectives for meditation, everyone follows the very same meditation, principles and road of advancement, and we will cover everything beginners need to know in this simple book. Just don't give up very quickly and say, "I can't meditate" or "It doesn't suit me" before you give it a proper go. While we understand the frustration of wanting very quick results, it is that frustration of wanting instant results that is part of everyone's problem. The frantic pace of society is leading us all to experience higher levels of stress and anxiety, and due to these influences even our children can no longer concentrate for long periods of time. Because of the internet age, they are now have very short attention spans and because of impatience expect instant results. Do not adopt their errors into your own life. Since meditation is one of the cures for these ills, we should all start learning meditation as a necessary skill to counter these challenges.

When you first start practicing meditation in watching your mind, thoughts will definitely seem as if they are running all over the place. For many practitioners it will seem as if you cannot focus or concentrate on anything at all for any length of time, and you cannot keep your mind fixed with stability on any one topic. Your mind will seem scattered. This busyness of wandering thoughts is an apt description of an ordinary person's mind. Most people don't know that this is what their mind is actually like until they bother to sit down and really observe their mental state during meditation practice. That's when they first begin to see the scope of the problem for the first time. It's the first time they become aware of how easily distracted they become.

As soon as people who try to practice meditation first sit down, an internal dialogue also often starts running around in their head. It typically goes something like this: "Ok, my eyes are closed and it's dark. Now what? What am I supposed to be doing again? What did my teacher say? Hey, my arm itches ... should I scratch it? No, the teacher said I am supposed to sit here quietly and focus on watching my breath. How do I actually do that? Do I focus on the breath in my nostrils, or in my lungs? Does that mean I should focus on the in and out movement of the air from the lungs? Geez, I wish someone would tell me all

7

these things. Wait a second … I once heard somewhere that I should count my breath. Yeah, that's right, so should I start doing that now or wait until later? Wait a minute … that would busy my mind so why did someone say that? My breath is supposed to get calmer as I relax but I don't notice any difference at all. How many minutes has it already been? I've probably been at this at least 15 minutes already because my legs hurt, so maybe it is even longer. Okay, let me open my eyes to take a peek to see how long it's been and then I can adjust myself at the same time because I'm uncomfortable. Dang, it's only been eight minutes! I really hope this session ends soon and the teacher starts talking again."

This is how the mind works. Like a monkey which jumps from branch to branch, but in this case it jumps from thought to thought. It cannot settle down and clear itself of disturbances because it is always being drawn into a force-field of distractions that is stronger than your good intentions. We are always getting drawn into following the sensations of our bodies, or lose ourselves in a stream of wandering thoughts. We get lost in following daydreams or distractions. We cannot maintain a clear mind that just knows our thoughts, but always end up get entangled in various thought streams, thereby losing our state of naturally centered presence.

Thus when you are sitting in meditation as a beginner and discover your mind is jumping all over the place, you must understand that this is normal. This is to be expected. It is actually a sign of progress that you can finally notice this because normally you just get sucked into going along with all those thoughts and never notice anything at all. That's the definition of mental restlessness, scattering and distraction. You become entangled with all your thought streams and lose yourself. You lose your stable sense of presence.

After a bit of practice, however, you will start noticing this tendency for the very first time because you will finally be quiet enough to observe it. That awareness of the problem is good because *awareness is the first step to the solution of any issue*. Now you are finally observing your mind and noticing that it is wandering here and there without stop. Hence, awareness is the first step to making progress in settling your mind. Awareness is itself the practice of meditation.

Hence, mental busyness is where *everyone* starts and it is normal to notice it, but noticing the problem does not mean that you cannot meditate. It just means you have already improved your powers of awareness! You have already stated to cultivate a greater presence of mind, which is the basis, purpose and method of meditation practice. You are already becoming more centered even though you haven't yet noticed that result. Clear awareness, which is introspection of your mind, is what you always try to cultivate in meditation.

All meditation exercises involve cultivating clear awareness just like this, and you don't have to create awareness because awareness is always naturally there. You just have to learn how to use the awareness of your mind properly. If your awareness becomes clear, then it becomes easy to concentrate. Therefore you need to learn how to focus your awareness or attention on thoughts without getting entangled in those thoughts and losing yourself. Most meditation methods involve focusing on different types of mental factors, with detachment, so that your mind stays clear but also abides on that object of attention without straying. You learn how to cultivate stable awareness without distraction.

Meditation is considered *mind training* because you train your awareness and powers of concentration. You learn how to properly use your mind's inherent power of awareness, which is learning how to properly use the mind itself! When you learn something like logic, or how to make comparisons or inferences, these are particular types of mental skills or functions of the mind you learn to master. With meditation you learn how to use the mind itself, which is simply a vehicle of awareness, rather than how to properly produce specific types of thoughts or perform certain mental functions.

Your progress along these lines will be swift if you follow the simple instructional guidelines in this book. Starting with just a little practice effort you will eventually achieve a lot. You already have everything you need, and just need to learn how to use the observation or witnessing powers of your mind differently. The way you use your mind now is already fraught with wrong habits.

Through meditation practice you will simply learn how to use its powers of awareness differently, namely *correctly*. Then you will find that your mind is naturally clear and free of distracting thoughts, and you can always know whatever thoughts arise without it overly troubling you. You'll learn how to tap into a deep calmness of the mind while knowing all the thoughts that arise within it. Progress always starts with tiny steps, so to achieve this you just have to start practicing and then let the fruits of attainment grow naturally. You cannot force meditation progress, but you can definitely achieve progress quicker through more practice effort.

Hundreds of millions of people across the world have learned how to meditate, and if they have done so then so can you. It's like learning to drive a car (or even riding a bicycle) where everything seems entirely new and different and a little frightening or difficult at first, but with a little time the skill becomes second nature.

The point is, just remember that training your mind to learn meditation takes some gentle persistence of practice effort. If you adopt the habit of consistent meditation practice, you will certainly gain all the benefits you have heard about.

2
SOME BASIC PRINCIPLES

Before we get into the details of how to meditate, we want you to understand some basic theory about meditation. It is very rare that anyone explains these basic principles, but you need to know these simple facts in order to make as much progress as quickly as possible.

Cessation and Observation

The first point is that all meditation methods in the world, and in fact all genuine spiritual practices, depend on two basic principles for training the mind. These two principles are called "**cessation**" and "**observation**." Their meaning is very easy to understand.

The idea of **cessation** is that your mind will eventually quiet down because of meditation practice. It will calm down when you learn how to let go of clinging to your thoughts. Before you learn how to meditate, your mind is usually running all over the place. However, after you start learning meditation then your mind will start to calm down, but this result takes time and effort to achieve. If wandering thoughts calm down it means they stop arising, and that stopping is called cessation.

The rule of progress for meditation, or for mastering any skill, is that:

Practice + Consistent Effort + Time = Result

What this means is that you must correctly practice meditation without interruptions, and with a positive attitude of patience and vigor, and over time you will achieve the results of mental calming. You will certainly gain the results you are seeking, but that achievement doesn't happen instantly.

To practice correctly, whenever you find your mind straying and that you have lost your focus during some type of meditation, you must bring your focus back to the task of meditation once again. "Consistent effort" means diligence over time with persistence, and being diligent during your practice sessions as well. You must bring your attention back to the task of meditation whenever it strays until mental focus and concentration become a consistent habit. If you continue to do this over a long period of time when you practice meditation with regularity, this is the meaning of practice and diligent effort.

No one achieves the experience of a quiet and clear mind right away when they start to meditate for the first few times, so you have to learn how to slowly achieve mental purity through consistent practice. Internal peace and serenity don't come from blanking out your thoughts or pushing them away but by watching them without getting involved with them and then they naturally calm down. When you just witness your thought stream without getting entangled with those thoughts, it is the same as not feeding them any energy. Without feeding them further

13

energy, they will slowly dissipate and reach a state of cessation where they are no longer there and the mind is clear. Therefore you just practice knowing them (watching them or being observant of them like a third person observer) and that is enough.

If you don't feed your thoughts any energy to further develop a particular thought stream, then what is in your mind right now will simply depart and be replaced by something else. The proven promise of meditation is that if you just keep letting go of your thoughts and refuse to attach to them then the internal noise level of thoughts in your head will calm down over time. Wandering thoughts that distract you will stop arising with abundance, and thus your mind will become more clear and peaceful. When you learn how to let go of thoughts, fewer and fewer random thoughts will arise in your mind. These results are the meaning of "cessation," which is to cultivate a quieter mind that is empty of random wandering thoughts.

This result of cessation follows the same principle used in managing a fire; a fire exhausts itself without any fuel, and so if you refuse to feed your thoughts energy because you refuse to get overly entangled with them (and just observe them or know them), your internal thought spinning nature will spontaneously come to rest. That quieting is cessation. Thoughts will spontaneously come to a rest if you just watch them with detachment, and that is the practice of meditation.

Meditation practice is therefore like a mom who takes her children to the playground and sits on the bench watching them play on their own, but without getting involved in their activities. In time her children will get tired all by themselves, and then they will want to fall asleep when they run out of energy. Hence, through meditation practice your mental scenario will become clear and peaceful without any effort done on your part except the patient witnessing of your thoughts … just knowing them without attaching to them. In meditation we say you should not "cling to" or "attach to" thoughts, which some schools describe by saying you should practice "detachment." Detachment doesn't mean you don't care or are indifferent, but simply means you aren't clinging to your mental realm.

When your thoughts quiet down, this means there is no longer a high degree of disturbing or wandering thoughts running around in your head. Your head is more empty of wandering thoughts, and thus you have greater powers of concentration because you aren't overwhelmed by busyness and random distractions. That is the definite result of meditation, which is why you want to practice in the first place. If your mind becomes quiet, it is because this volume of wandering thoughts has decreased. Because there are less wandering thoughts you can then start to experience the internal peace, quiet, silence, serenity, or tranquility which are the promise of meditation practice.

Once again, that internal quiet, or absence of thoughts, is called "cessation" or "stopping" because wandering thoughts have *stopped*. They have *ceased*. They have spontaneously come to rest, and that is why your mind now seems quiet. You certainly will still have thoughts arising whenever you need them, but the degree of random or wandering thoughts is reduced. Therefore you attain a more empty mind of clarity and concentration. Your mind becomes quiet.

In yoga this is called "cessation of the movements of the mind" and it simply means that your wandering thoughts have calmed down. Your mind has become empty of random thoughts and that quiet state is called quieting, calming or cessation. In Christianity, this exact same result is called "silence," "peace," "stillness," "centering" or "serenity" but those are just different words used to describe the very same result of cessation.

Some spiritual schools call this quietness "emptiness" because a quiet mind seems as if it is empty, and once again these are different words for exactly the same meaning. In Judaism we say that "thoughts become annihilated" and thinking experiences "nothingness," so the result is once again emptiness or the absence of thoughts described differently. In Buddhism, achieving a quiet mind is simply called "calming" or that you achieve a state of "calm abiding." There are so many synonyms, but everyone is pointing to the exact same end result. If you just watch your thoughts without getting involved with them, they will calm down and your mental realm will become clear and clean, pure and pacified.

You can call the quiet state you reach from meditation by many names such as silence, peace, quiet, quiescence, purity, tranquility, emptiness, calming, cessation, stopping, resting, no mind, no thoughts and so forth. This is the goal of meditation practice, and spiritual practices as well. You basically want to reach a state of internal mental peace and quiet through your meditation practice, and that state is called "cessation" because most random, wandering thoughts have disappeared. Hence the first principle you must understand is that meditation helps you reach a state where wandering thoughts are absent, and that resultant empty quiet state is called "stopping" or "cessation." We like to simply say that your mind becomes "more empty."

Now we can move onto the second big principle of meditation practice. The second point to understand is that when you reach a state where your mind becomes quiet because of your meditation practice, you still want to remain aware and awake during that state. You are not supposed to slip into a trance, dull your senses, suppress your thinking process, or try to enter into a sleepy or confused state of mind where you seem to be thinking less because you are holding onto a state of ignorance. Rather, you are to remain open, clean, bright, aware, attentive and awake. You remain aware of your mind, but just don't cling to whatever arises within it. That awareness is called "observation."

With meditation you are *cultivating awareness* because you want to know your mind clearly. Yes, you want disturbing random thoughts to settle, but you also want to be cultivating clear awareness, which is a point people always tend to gloss over. You are NOT trying to cultivate dullness or unknowingness. You want to definitely know all your thoughts, as they come and go, and that state of aliveness is called observation, watching or witnessing. If we didn't have this knowingness we would be inert and insentient, so awareness is a basic aspect of existence we don't want to try to annihilate.

In meditation practice, your mind quiets and yet you stay aware witnessing your mind. You don't push thoughts away through suppression, or attach to them with clinging, but just let them come and go without interference while knowing them. This is being perfectly natural without any stress. You know things with detachment.

Observing or **witnessing** your mind is therefore the second of the two principles inherent within every meditation practice. Together with cessation, these two principles always go together. Sometimes observation is called "cultivating awareness" or "concentration" or "attention," but the point is that you never want to be dulling your mind or suppressing your thoughts during meditation to produce mental peace. Rather, you always want to remain clear and *aware* in your mind without pushing thoughts in any way, even if your mind is busy, so you always want to just let thoughts come and go without clinging to them. If you learn how to do this while remaining attentive with witnessing, over time the level of internal dis-quiet in your mind will decrease. That is a rule you can depend upon.

For instance, a child might play on a swing set and push their legs off the ground in conjunction with the rhythm of the swing to make it go higher and higher. This is like adding energy to your thought processes to keep a train of thoughts going, and that entanglement makes thought streams continue longer. If the child didn't keep feeding that pendulum motion energy, then in time it would die down quite naturally. Similarly, instead of just watching their mind and knowing their thoughts, people always get very entangled with their consciousness, add energy in every direction, and then get lost in tangles of confusion. They feed energy to the "monkey mind" that jumps from thought to thought without end.

This is called "following thoughts," "getting entangled" with them, or "cultivating a mind of confusion" rather than just observing them, watching them, witnessing them, being aware of them, or knowing them. It is because people become overly involved with their thought streams that they get lost, and then wandering thoughts continue to proliferate within their minds. Meditation teaches you how to take a break from this habit and just practice mental resting while you remain your natural self.

Thoughts will always naturally arise effortlessly in your mind without any effort necessary on your part, and then they will also disappear without any effort required because they cannot stay. This is the natural way consciousness functions; thoughts cannot stay but must leave, and therefore you need not do anything to make them leave. A stream of thoughts arises only for as long as it is needed, and then they depart. Therefore you don't have to try to push them away because they simply cannot stay.

Because most *wandering* thoughts which arise are not needed, it is easy for them to subside if we don't give that particular thought stream undue attention. And when many wandering thoughts subside, the mind is left alone in a state of vivid clarity, which we call pristine awareness. This is what we try to cultivate in meditation. You can say we are trying to cultivate the absence of thoughts, or cessation, or say we are trying to cultivate this clarity, or pure awareness. We want to get to that state because it is peaceful and clear rather than full of disturbances, annoyances or distractions. The problem is that wandering thoughts stand in our way of experiencing this, and we never reduce the level of these mental distractions because we have an ingrained habit of clinging to our own consciousness.

A pristine awareness is always there in your mind which allows you to know things, so it is not something that you create. Rather, this clear awareness is always covered by thought attachments, and so that we never notice it. We are always attaching to thoughts, and this habit blinds us and obscures it. Your ordinary mind is like an empty awareness, and thoughts simply arise within it. Those thoughts are not you but just things that appear within your mind. The substance of your mind, which is part of you, is that empty awareness and it is absolutely ordinary. It isn't anything special. It is perfectly natural and ordinary.

Because ordinary people never observe their minds, they don't realize these simple facts unless they start to practice meditation. Only meditation can lead you to this type of realization. During meditation practice, you always want to just watch your thoughts without getting mixed up with them and further attach to whatever is obscuring the your clear mind of awareness. You have to train you mind to be like a mirror that lets images arise within it, but doesn't cling to them in any way. You want to know your own mind with clarity without losing a sense of presence.

When you are falling asleep at the wheel of a car and try to pull yourself out of sleepiness into a zone of wakefulness, that momentary state of clearness and brightness you attain, before succumbing to lethargy once again, is your clear awareness. You momentarily attain a state of presence, bright mind, or pristine awareness that is itself silent, and this is what you can cultivate through meditation.

Your mental awareness is something that never moves whereas everything else that moves within the mind is a thought (manifest consciousness). The part of consciousness that doesn't move but is there all the time is called awareness, pure consciousness or illumination, and in meditation you want to cultivate staying in that clear aspect of consciousness. You stay in an unmoving state while the moving scenery of mental phenomena pass by. You want to practice staying in the pristine awareness that knows manifest consciousness without ever falling into those thought streams. It knows them but always stays independent of them.

Just as the pendulum motion of a swing set will die down if you don't feed it any energy, so will any streams of random thoughts die down if you just stay centered in awareness and watch them without getting sucked into them. In learning how to meditate you will reach a point where mental busyness naturally diminishes, and then that calmness can be carried into regular life. Always just let your thoughts arise and depart, and simply know them without attaching to them. This is called cultivating a bright mind or mind of bright awareness. So there is a saying, "Meditation is cultivating a bright mind of awareness."

Whenever you need a thought, it will always arise. It has been this way all your life, hasn't it? It is a rule of nature. Your thoughts won't always be correct, but consciousness calls forth the appropriate thoughts due to circumstances, so thoughts will always arise when you need them such as when you want to focus your thinking in some direction. When you hear a bird song you immediately know it's a bird because your thoughts instantly arise due to the sounds, and consciousness will always call forth the best thoughts it can like this when you need them.

The arising of thoughts according to circumstances is an unbreakable law of consciousness, so you don't have to worry you will stop thinking because of meditation. Thoughts will always arise. You should let thoughts arise, but simply refuse to attach to the thoughts that arise because you want to stay centered in awareness. While you may think you never attach to thoughts, you have developed a subtle habit of clinging to your manifest consciousness and this habit is so ingrained that we don't even notice it any longer because it has been there for so long. You will finally learn how to break this habit through the practice of meditation.

Therefore you should always feel free to let go of your consciousness when meditating because you won't ever miss anything. Thoughts will always arise when you need them. Nothing will disappear. Consciousness will always be there, and your awareness will be there as well as well. You won't in some way become annihilated or "disappear." It is the habit of clinging to consciousness that you want to get rid of while leaving anything else to the natural responses. Without the habit of mentally clinging to thoughts, your mind will still function but it will seem clear, calm, peaceful and bright. Thus, people think meditation practice is something mysterious, but you are simply cultivating your ordinary mind. You are simply cultivating the awareness you already naturally have. Your mind doesn't turn into anything else, but just loses all sorts of layers of pollution when you let go of clinging to them. Then unnecessary layers of pollution will stop arising.

Some people mistakenly worry they will somehow stop thinking and have no thoughts at all from meditation, but it's impossible to become like that. Thoughts will always arise, but the internal level of distracting, random, wandering thoughts will decline because of meditation practice, and then you will know mental clarity. Therefore, over time your mind will become pure and clean and your thinking more sharp and penetrating because there aren't any random distractions. You will become able to concentrate, with clarity and stability, for longer and longer periods of time after much practice.

Meditation does not mean to cultivate a state of mental blankness to achieve cessation. It does not mean suppressing thoughts using force, or pushing them away to produce a state of mental torpor. It just means to learn how to let go of thoughts, let go of your thought streams, let go of manifest consciousness while letting it function freely without interference. If you learn how to break these ingrained habits of clinging to consciousness, then wandering thought waves will subside and you will slowly become able to access an underlying realm of clarity that has always been there. You can then take that mental peace and quiet you earn from meditation into the regular world.

In movies you might see an aged Zen monk whose mind seems alert, calm, open and relaxed, and that's the state you want to reach through meditation. You want to cultivate this type of clear, clean awareness that doesn't hold onto thoughts, and incorporate it together with your activities the real world.

Hence the two principles inherent in all meditation practices are cessation and observation. You perform some type of meditation practice and then your mind eventually quiets down. It reaches a state of cessation where the mental busyness passes away, but you aren't falling into a trance or falling asleep. You aren't trying to suppress your thoughts or obstruct them in any way. You are not trying to cultivate a dull state of mind, which is hazy in some way, by suppressing thoughts to artificially bring about mental quiet. You are not trying to go into a trance, or dull your mind, or practice some strange form of hypnosis. You are simply resting your mind of its tendency to cling to all forms of consciousness, including the entire body of consciousness itself, and your mind will then naturally become clear.

You simply let go of thoughts and they just die down naturally to produce a state of quiet calming, or cessation. That mental state is very calm, comfortable, peaceful and clear. Your mind is now more "clear" because it is free of distracting or random thoughts. It is still just your ordinary mind, but is clear of all sorts of random pollutions. Hence, even though you have reached cessation, there is still witnessing, awareness or observation.

Now, because of meditation practice, you are even more

fit for doing all your activities in the real world. You still know everything that goes through your mind but your awareness doesn't cling to whatever mentally arises. You become capable of handling more tasks with better proficiency because of greater clarity and abilities of concentration. You just know everything that goes on in your mind clearly but you stay detached from whatever arises in that you don't cling to it. Detachment doesn't mean indifference (that you don't care) or not having emotions, but that you simply do not try to cling to whatever consciousness arises.

Witnessing or observation means that your awareness remains active within that state of calm and clarity. Therefore we say that your mind remains "bright" rather than that it becomes dulled by the effort of seeking quiet by thought suppression. You stay fully awake and aware while meditating and always continue to know all the contents of your mind clearly. *This is the rule for all meditation practices!*

Witnessing or observation practice is like a person who sees his friends drive by in a car waving at him. He continues standing at the edge of the road witnessing everything, but he doesn't focus on following them down the road while ignoring everything else. He doesn't let them overly capture his attention so that he gets sucked into following them and then ignores everything else going on. He does not get "pulled into" following any particular train of thought and then lose his presence of mind. That's the principle of observation or watching the mind in meditation practice.

When we say that the mind becomes "empty" or reaches cessation it means that wandering thoughts become fewer in number, but it does not mean that thoughts do not arise. You still know them, but "emptiness" means both a reduction in their volume and the fact that you are independent of them because you are free of mental clinging. Mental clinging has become emptied or non-existent. Thoughts cannot pull you into their stream, and so you stay as their master, the host of these guests. Your awareness thereby stays crisp, pure and clean. In this way, meditation practice involves both principles of cessation and observation.

It takes time to master these two principles through meditation practice. Our mental habit is that we are easily sucked into scenarios where we lose our state of "presence" due to thought entanglements, and thus cannot reach cessation. With meditation we must learn to know our thoughts while always remaining clear and independent, which is observation.

Contemplation and Wisdom

Until you start to meditate with regularity, you may not recognize that your mind is always moving. It is never still and clear but always involved with thinking, jumping from thought to thought, and in particular is prone to two types of states: restlessness and distraction, or torpor and sleepiness. When we are awake our thoughts constantly scatter and envelop the mind with restlessness, like a monkey which jumps from branch to branch, until we fall asleep at night and retire into unconsciousness.

Even during the day we can fall into states of sleepiness, haziness, lethargy and unclearness. Therefore we are always experiencing one of these two states of either mental excitedness or torpor. If intensified, these states may turn into mental disorders which is why there is a call for meditation in the world so that we can rest the mind from busyness and cultivate peace and clarity.

Thus this brings up a third and fourth principle that you often hear about when it comes to meditation practice. These are the principles of "**contemplation**" (mental analysis) and "**wisdom**" (insight).

Some types of meditation practice ask you to observe your wandering thoughts and then from this observation try to analyze the nature of consciousness and your mind. They ask you to look within to watch where your thoughts come from and go to, and to examine the nature of your mind, so that you can make conclusions about what you find.

If you watch your thought stream, analyze what you see and start making logical conclusions, this is called contemplation, analysis, examination or discrimination that can result in understanding, insight, recognition, realization or wisdom about the nature of thoughts and your mind. You observe your mind during quiet meditation and with logic come to various conclusions such as the fact that your thoughts come and go without ceasing and are birthed in an endless stream where each thought arises because of a dependence on the prior thoughts that came before it. This type of analysis of consciousness (which comes from observing your mind) is a meditation practice in itself, and is called "contemplation." You look directly at your mind and try to fathom the nature of consciousness.

Thus, the second set of meditation principles you often hear about involve applying **contemplation** (analysis or discrimination) to consciousness itself to arrive at **insight** (wisdom, understanding or realization) about the nature and functioning of your mind. If you look directly at your mind and analyze it, you can come to some realizations about its true nature.

When did anyone ever teach you how to do this in life? In religion they teach you about various dogmas, but they never teach you to find the root of your consciousness which is somehow connected with your true self. Through meditation, however, you can directly discover the nature of your mind and the ultimate source behind consciousness and your self. Therefore the major purpose of contemplation practice is to help you realize the nature of this thing called "consciousness" we all have. We use it everyday, but not once are we ever told to analyze this thing called "consciousness" that is giving us beingness, our existence, and the world. If you start to unravel the mystery of consciousness through contemplation, you should know that this is the basis of all higher spiritual practices. If you go so far as to find the source of consciousness, you actually succeed in spiritual cultivation because there is no higher realization in the universe.

When you contemplate the nature of your mind by directly looking at your consciousness and making conclusions about its nature, you will certainly develop more spiritual understanding than you can ordinarily find through religion. Some meditation schools use a special term for these types of insight and say that when you analyze your mind or mind stream, then *"prajna **wisdom**"* will be born. Prajna wisdom is a special type of understanding about the nature of your mind.

"Prajna" means transcendental and refers to any understandings or realizations about the fundamental nature of your mind. Your true mind, or the true nature of your mind, is called "transcendental" because it is beyond phenomena. It is beyond phenomena (transcending them) because they appear within it. Since it is beyond the forms of manifest consciousness that appear within it, it is not anything phenomenal itself. Thus we have several reasons for the term *"prajna* transcendental wisdom" which refers to developing understanding about the characteristics and substance of your mind.

You can develop wisdom understanding about all sorts of topics, but *"prajna* wisdom" is the highest type of wisdom because it means understanding the transcendental nature of the root source of your consciousness, which is actually understanding your beingness or true level of existence. The highest type of *prajna* transcendental wisdom means understanding, through direct experience, the one ultimate reality that is the absolute ground state of our consciousness and beingness. It means understanding, because of direct experience, the ultimate root source of all matter and consciousness in the universe! Because this target is so high, we call this a spiritual or "transcendental" understanding and you can actually reach this understanding through meditation practice. That is why meditation is used as a spiritual practice.

Many people are interested in meditation for spiritual progress, and those are the people who must learn how to analyze the mind and cultivate *prajna* wisdom to arrive at this type of realization. When you find the root source of all matter and conscious in the universe, it is called enlightenment, self-realization, or attaining the Tao. Those who are just pursuing meditation for health and longevity purposes rarely bother to study the nature of their mind because they are just interested in the benefits of mental calming and better health, but the highest levels of meditation practice are achieved when you try to cultivate this *prajna* wisdom. If you cultivate prajna wisdom through contemplation, you will get all the other benefits of health, vigor, mental calming and longevity along the way, so this should actually be your target. Reach for the stars and you can certainly attain the moon! All the meditation methods within this book lead to mental calming and better health, and if you pursue them diligently they can all lead you to a high degree of *prajna* transcendental wisdom.

For instance, when you look at your mind and observe the comings and goings of your thoughts during meditation, you will eventually realize that your mind is inherently empty. Its true nature is not moving thoughts but purity; the nature of consciousness is emptiness whereas its function is manifestation, and what appears are thoughts. As to the substance of your mind, it is of an insubstantial, non-phenomenal, unmanifest nature in that absolutely nothing is there. That's why we say it is empty or pure, and this is the nature of ordinary awareness. It never changes into anything else but always remains what it is.

However, within awareness thoughts continue to arise and

depart in an unbroken chain like an endless river, and within that ceaseless river the appearance of specific thoughts is due to a complex set of interdependent relationships which produces whatever arises. What arises within *your* mind is different than the reactions within my mind because of different memories, habits, and ways of seeing things. But whatever arises is due to complex cause and effect relationships.

Whether for you or me, a circumstance provokes a response, and then the appropriate thoughts arise in the mind. What arises within our minds might be a correct or incorrect conclusion, evil rather than good, logical or silly and so forth, but that's a function of our wisdom, virtue, merits, knowledge and training rather than the fact that the thought-birthing process is faulty. Who can predict exactly what will come up? What arises does so because of a complex set of relationships which even a supercomputer could not predict.

If you have ingrained habits of thinking, those habits will produce a certain characteristic type of thoughts, which is why you must practice virtuous ways if you want good thoughts to arise as a tendency. Now you can see the importance of training and education. You never have to worry about thoughts not arising for any situation, but you must worry that your knowledge, logic, virtue and wisdom are insufficient that better thoughts don't arise. You need never worry that thoughts might permanently disappear because of meditation practice and therefore that "you" might somehow become extinct or annihilated. Thoughts will always arise, and you simply want to cultivate a clear mind that does not cling to them. You always want to cultivate *clarity in knowing*, and as to the thoughts themselves, that is an issue of wisdom, skillfulness, knowledge, compassion, and virtue.

Thoughts are always born in your mind and then pass away. During meditation practice, you simply watch this process and detach from it, witnessing it like an independent third person observer who doesn't get entangled in whatever he observes. If, like a hotel concierge who stands motionless watching his lobby with all the guests coming in and going out, you just watch the thoughts pass through your mind without getting pulled into them, in time excessive wandering thoughts will quiet down and you will enjoy a very clear and bright mental state. Witnessing awareness stands outside this realm of manifest consciousness, and if you can learn how to rest in that pristine awareness, which is always clear and empty, then you can find the truest peace of meditation.

The manifest consciousness of thoughts is actually no different from this purest substance of the mind that is empty of all things, and this pure essence of consciousness is often called emptiness, pure consciousness, pristine awareness or illumination. To understand this topic is called "cultivating *prajna* wisdom" once again because it refers to understanding the nature of your mind. If you cultivate *prajna* wisdom you can penetrate through many of the strange notions held by the organized religions and see for yourself what is really true or false about the nature of your self. This task of mentally investigating what you truly are, by tracing your manifest consciousness back to its absolute purest primordial and fundamental origins, is called "spiritual cultivation."

Meditation, Breathing and Internal Energy

The last thing you should know about meditation practice is the sequence of progress that every practitioner passes through. The typical sequence of making progress is as follows.

You first practice some meditation technique. Your thoughts then start calming down. Your thoughts calm down because you just watch them like an independent third party observer who doesn't add any energy to the process but just witnesses events without getting involved. Therefore any lack of clarity within your mind caused by distracting wandering thoughts starts dissipating and you eventually reach an undisturbed state of internal quiet.

That quiet state of "empty mind" or cessation is peaceful and calm and clear, which is the target of meditation practice. Your mind remains clear and bright in that it is not dulled, but is vividly aware but quiet. Wandering thoughts that might have distracted you are now gone.

When you first start to reach this stage of mental emptiness, you might even notice that your mind seems busier than before and become worried that you are backsliding in progress. Like a glass of dirty water that has been stirred up, you only start seeing the individual particles of dust within that chaotic water when it finally starts to settle, so the fact that you can notice the busyness of your mind is due to progress from it becoming settled rather than the fact it is becoming busier.

As you continue to practice meditation by letting go of the endless stream of consciousness that goes by within your mind, your breathing will tend to slow down because your breathing and your thoughts (consciousness) are linked. As your thinking calms down so your breathing will calm down to become much more harmonious and balanced. Sometimes your breathing will soften so much that it even seems to stop for a short period of time during your meditation practice, and when that happens it is an excellent sign of progress.

This softening and slowing of your respiration can happen when your real internal energy, the life force of your body, finally begins to become activated through meditation. This is our target objective if we want to become healthier and live longer, or if we want to cultivate meditation for spiritual purposes. Spiritual progress depends on that internal energy as well. As this vital energy becomes activated and starts to flow throughout your body, you don't need to rely on external respiration as much and all your organ functions become healthier and more efficient.

The arising of that internal energy, known as **chi** or **prana** or **kundalini**, is how meditation rejuvenates your body. As your mind quiets the real life force or internal energy inside you comes up and that energy will subsequently open up all your acupuncture meridians, called "*chi* channels."

This new energy flowing inside you produces a type of internal rejuvenation and renewal. In fact, as the *chi* channels within your brain start opening due to meditation practice, then through them will flow a much smoother circulation of *chi*. Because the *chi* flow within your brain becomes smoother, and because that energy flow is connected with the arising of thoughts, this is why the reduction of random thoughts becomes somewhat permanent, where you can take that clarity with you into the regular world, when you start practicing meditation.

The scientific principle that this all depends upon is that your breathing and consciousness are linked. Even science recognizes that breathing and consciousness (thoughts) are interconnected. For instance, if your breathing becomes scattered then your mind can become wild. If your breathing becomes calm then your mind will become peaceful. When frightened your breathing quickens and it calms as your mind becomes more peaceful.

You can therefore calm your breathing to help calm your mind, or by calming your mind through meditation practice you will in turn calm your respiration. The most interesting thing is that when you calm your breathing and it slows to what seems like a halt, your internal energy will start arising within your body, and many people will begin to feel these internal energies.

If your internal energy starts to arise due to cultivating meditation, yoga, martial arts or other relevant practices, then over time your body will soften and become warmer. Your circulation will get better and your energy will increase. You will also start to feel more blissful and alive inside. That energy, left alone to circulate by itself without any interference from your mind, will then open up all your internal energy meridians to produce such results.

There are many teachings on how you can cultivate this internal energy, but this is a basic beginner's book on meditation, so for more instructions on this matter you can turn to some of the recommended books in the appendix. Individuals who are very advanced along these lines but want to learn more are especially encouraged to read *The Little Book of Hercules*, and if you want instructions for reaching this stage you should turn to *The Little Book of Meditation*.

Conclusion

These are the basic principles of meditation practice you should know:

- All meditation practices involve the two principles of cessation and observation.

- Contemplating the nature of your mind during mentally quiet states leads to a special type of wisdom.

- Meditation practice slows your breathing, calms your mind, and also affects the internal vital energy currents within your body.

These are very simple principles, yet few people are ever taught these things. These principles are the basis of human being science, which involves the task of cultivating oneself to become a better human being, but few are ever taught such basic life principles.

Thus it is said that there are four difficult things in the universe. To become a human being, to be born in a civilized society, to meet with an enlightened master, and to come in touch with real cultivation teachings. If you understand these principles and match them with your meditation practice, this understanding is sure to help your practice blossom.

3
HOW TO SIT PROPERLY

You will often see people sitting in a strange position for meditation called the "full lotus" posture. Do you have to use that position to meditate? No, of course not, but there are very good reasons people sit in this special position and why this is the first posture that practitioners usually try to learn.

In ancient India many people practiced sitting meditation throughout their lives using the lotus posture, where the legs are crossed and folded on top of one another, to do so. While the "full lotus" posture you often see used in yoga classes has been the general meditation posture used in the East for millennia, it often isn't easy for Westerners to get used to this special position because they usually have stiffer joints and are not used to sitting on the ground. Rather than the full lotus posture, most Westerners usually prefer sitting cross-legged in a "half lotus" position for meditation.

The lotus sitting posture was actually developed out of physiological considerations because that special sitting position helps to enhance the flow of your physical body's internal energy, and it also facilitates concentration power. You can find ancient Indian books where yoga enthusiasts tried out all sorts of different sitting postures for meditation and tested them for their effectiveness in mental calming and internal energy flow. They found that the lotus sitting posture was the best position possible of all others in allowing your body to find a stable position it could maintain for a long period of time, and for holding the body's energies inside so that they don't scatter but can be channeled inwards for spiritual, mental or physical benefits.

In short, the lotus posture is the best sitting position ever found that allows you to remain motionless for a long period of time without using a lot of energy to maintain that stable position. Furthermore, that special position facilitates the relaxation of your body, the free flow of energy throughout your body, and the energizing of your brain because it allows your internal energies to flow unrestrictedly into your head. During meditation practice you want to remain clearheaded, rather than fall into sleepiness or torpor, so this posture helps you fulfill this requirement as well. As you can see, there are countless benefits to mastering this position, which is why most people choose to learn it.

In order to sit in a full lotus posture, both of your legs should cross one another at the calf. Both of your feet should rest on the opposite thighs and your knees should be touching the ground. As to your hands, they should rest naturally in your lap on top of each other with palms facing upward. The tips of the thumbs should slightly touch one another, which connects opposite areas of the brain.

You can put the left hand on top of the right, but traditionally people rest the right hand on top of the left. Some people say you should put the left hand on top of the right if your left leg is crossing on top of the right, and put the right hand on top if the right leg is crossing on top of the left leg. The rule you should use is to just find a position where your hands feel natural and unforced with thumbs lightly touching.

Now for your back and shoulders. Many people have seen pictures of Japanese Zen monks sitting in meditation with spines as erect and straight as a board. They actually are using force to be this straight, and this is incorrect because they are using energy to maintain a position that should exist naturally. If they hold their back too straight though excessive effort, their energy cannot flow freely up the spine into the brain. Hence your back should be held straight, but remain soft and flexible. You don't want to be slouching when you are practicing meditation.

When you are sitting in meditation, everything should be natural. Your head, neck, and your spine should certainly lie in a vertical line when you are sitting, but they don't have to be held perfectly straight because your spine should assume its natural curve that is like a bow. Your shoulders should be held erect so that they are not drooping, but you shouldn't be holding them with effort either. Your chest should be open and relaxed.

Your chin should be slightly pulled back, which puts pressure on the two large arteries in the neck, and you should close the eyes or keep them slightly open to prevent drowsiness. Your face should be relaxed instead of held tightly, and there should be a light smile on your face. Your upper and lower lips should lightly touch one another, and your tongue should touch the upper teeth at the roof of the mouth. Advanced practitioners can curl their tongue backwards to touch their palate. The purpose of all these instructions is to find a position that is comfortable and which you can maintain without using force so that you can forget the body altogether when you are meditating.

Your spine should certainly be held upright without leaning to the left or right when you are meditating, but it is okay for it to bend a little like a bow because you want to be relaxed. In time it will become straighter just by itself as your internal energy starts to flow through it because of better practice. However, at the beginning when you are first learning how to sit properly, you simply want to get into a stable position you can maintain that feels relaxed. To feel relaxed when you are sitting, take off your glasses, unbuckle your belt, remove your watch and loosen your clothing to attain that state of comfort.

If possible, you can try to sit for meditation practice without using a pillow or cushion underneath your buttocks. Flexible people usually don't need to sit on a pillow or cushion whereas people with stiffer joints or who are very large should use one. Sitting on the edge of a cushion helps to both elevate and straighten your spine and it also helps you maintain your balance during sitting so that you don't feel like you will fall over. This is one of the superior advantages of the lotus position. When you are sitting, some people also use a towel to cover their knee joints (or neck) to protect themselves from drafts.

As a beginning meditator you should certainly try using the full lotus posture where you cross your legs on top of one another, with your feet on your opposite calves, to see what it is like. If the position is too uncomfortable or produces numbness and tingling in the legs, you can try a half lotus posture where just one leg and foot lies on the calf of the other leg while the other is uncrossed and outstretched. Each time you practice you can start off using the full lotus position and then switch to a more comfortable position, such as the half lotus, when it becomes too uncomfortable. This is how to master it over time.

In other words, if the full lotus position feels too tight or uncomfortable, then just release that position and use a posture where just one leg is crossed and the other rests comfortably in front of you. Or, you can sit with both legs resting on top of one another without being locked on the hips. There are many sitting positions you can use. The point is to find a position with your back straight that is comfortable so that you can eventually forget your body during practice, but your position should still be stable enough that you don't fall over and you don't need a lot of energy to maintain it.

Remember that *you are not practicing yoga but meditation*, and since during meditation you want to be relaxed and let go of your body, you need to find a stable position that is easy on your joints and easy to maintain. That's the principle, so don't be straining yourself to maintain a painful position if it is distracting you from your practice. You shouldn't force yourself to stay in a full lotus sitting position if all you are doing during your meditation session is thinking about how painful or uncomfortable it is.

On the other hand, you do want to slowly train yourself to get used to this position over time. We may suffer some slight discomfort from trying to master the lotus position, but the eventual outcome is that we will triumph over the pain and in time achieve the freedom of spirit we all desire.

If your legs often fall asleep or become numb from this position, it indicates that your blood circulation within these limbs is already not in good condition, so learning this posture will actually force your circulation to become better. Some people use the natural supplement *nattokinase* to help dissolve any internal blood clots within their arteries and veins, and this often surprisingly eliminates pain and discomfort in parts of the body afflicted with poor circulation.

As you practice a full or half lotus position for some time, your knee joints will definitely become more supple and the position will become much easier to maintain over time. The main rule is to be at ease and thoroughly relaxed in your muscles, nerves, and brain when you are sitting.

Noises and bright lights may create tension when you are trying to meditate while darkness may cause sleepiness, so for the best practice results you will also want to sit in a room or environment that has minimal distractions. You should also avoid sitting in front of a draft, open window or air conditioner when meditating. You should always avoid sitting directly in front of drafts during meditation practice, and Chinese medicine warns that this is a rule for lovemaking as well. Lastly, people most often close their eyes when meditating, but some find it easier to partially open their eyes, so it is up to you to discover what works best.

A general rule is that it is better to meditate often for a shorter period of time than to meditate infrequently but for a long period of time. To make real progress, meditation should become a vital part of your daily life, and that often requires that you schedule it into your daily routine.

4
YOUR FIRST BASIC MEDITATION

We are now ready to learn a very simple meditation method. Since this is a very simple method, to learn it you can sit in any posture that helps your mind become quiet. Just sit in a position where your body isn't tense but feels relaxed with your head erect. That's step one.

To practice this meditation technique and get the very best results, you will have to next adjust your breathing. That is the big secret to getting the quickest results of mental calming through meditation: adjust your breathing at the start of your practice session.

If you first adjust your breathing to calm down, then your mind can quickly enter a deep state of quiet because of the connection between your breathing and your thoughts. Calming your breath calms your mind, so to touch mental peace you first want to harmonize your breathing. Therefore before you start to meditate, you are first going to perform some deep inhalations and exhalations of your breath to let go of any tensions inside your body and mind. You will initially adjust your *chi*, breathing, body and mind in this way.

Here's how to do it …

You are going to breath in through your nose and then exhale *slowly* through your mouth, and do this 3-5 times in a row. You don't want to use any excessive force in doing this because you want to be natural about it, but you do want each of your exhalations to last longer than each inhalation.

There is one special principle to this initial phase of adjustment, which is that with every out-breath of exhalation it should be as if you are letting go of everything that might possibly be bothering you in the world, and you want to silently say "Ahhh" when you do this. Using these exhalations, you want to relax yourself by throwing away all your mental burdens.

For instance, imagine this scenario. Pretend you have been busy all day and you finally get a chance to sit down and relax. In front of you is a hot cup of tea, so you lean forward to take a sip. When it meets your lips you find out it's the perfect temperature and tastes absolutely delicious, so you lean back and breathe out saying "Ahhh." At that moment you breathe out and let go of everything in your mind, and feel absolutely perfect—even if it is for just a moment—because it is as if you have just shed a great burden off your shoulders. You have let go of everything and are finally enjoying yourself at the same time.

That's it. That's the initial preparatory adjustment for meditation. It sounds so simple, but most people do not first adjust their mind and body before when they sit in meditation, and then they wonder why they don't get any calming results.

Adjusting your breathing is one of the keys to being able to calm your mind quickly and then feel good during your practice session. If you do this first, then you won't have to spend the first portion of your sitting practice waiting for your internal energies to calm down so that your mind settles. You will be able to achieve some of those results just by going through this initial phase of adjustment.

You must first inhale air through your nose into your lungs, and then exhale *slowly* from your mouth to empty your lungs as if you are letting go of everything. Your exhalation should be about twice as long as the length of your inhalation, and you should let go of all your mental pressures and tensions upon those exhalations. Since you usually cannot do this with just one cycle of in and out respirations, it may take several repetitions to initially adjust yourself.

If you need more than 3-5 inhalations-exhalations to initially calm yourself down to adjust yourself, try inhaling for a count of four and then exhaling for a count of eight, and continue doing this several more times in a row following the same instructions. When exhaling, always remember to let go as if you are finally releasing a big burden off your shoulders, and it is as if "now life is perfect." Eventually you will reach a point where you feel like you have let go of everything, your body feels comfortable inside, and you can now begin practice.

After those adjustments, each time exhaling with a silent sound of "Ahhh" as if you are so happy to let go of everything in the world and release all your problems and pressures, close your mouth slightly with your tongue touching your upper teeth (or rolled backwards and touching the roof of your mouth for advanced practitioners). The point is to now adjust your mouth so that your face and head are relaxed.

Your mind should be quiet and a bit peaceful now. You should have entered a silent space just by virtue of the fact that you first adjusted your breathing to calm down, thus serving to harmonize the *chi* or internal energy of your body. This alone will produce a state that is somewhat mentally quiet. Now to deepen that state, you should just continue watching your breathing without getting involved with it. Then your breathing will further soften without becoming ruffled or perturbed, which would destroy any serenity you have achieved.

What do you do now? Just sit there pleasantly and start watching your breathing. You should follow what your breathing is doing with mental observation so that you know what's happening with your inhalations and exhalations, but you shouldn't interfere with your breathing process. You sit there comfortably and just know what is happening with your breathing without becoming involved with it. You let it operate automatically, and simply know what is happening as it moves in or out.

This is practicing awareness. You just follow your breathing with knowing, awareness, witnessing, observation or however you wish to word it. You don't try to guide it or quicken it or push it in any way, but just stay in that state of independent, detached observation and then your breathing will calm down and your mind will quiet down even more. That zone of quiet will eventually grow larger and become something you really enjoy.

Once you start to feel the calm in your mind, you will have then mastered the introductory basics of one type of meditation practice. If you cannot stay quiet inside … if your mind becomes busy again … then take another deep inhalation through your nose and then breathe out from your mouth very slowly, making a silent "Ahhh" sound while allowing the energy to rise into your head when you do so.

That's it. That's all you have to do. You have started to master one form of meditation practice. If you can only sit there quietly for 15-20 minutes, that's fine. If you can remain quiet for longer, that's even better. All you have to do is rest in the mental silence and when thoughts start to become busy again, take a deep inhalation and then exhale slowly. Let go of all your cares, let go of your body, and let your *chi* (internal energy) rise into your head with every deep exhalation.

Some teachers will tell you after you have adjusted your body and breathing that you should count your breaths or watch your thoughts as a type of meditation practice. Those are different meditation methods for cultivating concentration or awareness, and there are countless others are based on this first introductory practice of calming your mind and breathing. If you just start by learning this first basic technique, then you can slowly expand to try many other types of meditation practice. Go ahead and try it!

5
HOW TO MANTRA

Many meditation traditions teach people to recite mantras to calm their mind. Mantras are special phrases that may or may not have a special meaning, but certainly are composed of a special sequence of sounds that are very calming if you continually recite them.

The equivalent to mantra recitation in the Western religions is reciting prayers over and over again until the mind quiets and you reach a state of inner silence. Mantra recitation, called *"japa"* practice in India, accomplishes the same thing but in reciting a prayer you concentrate on holding to the meaning of the words whereas with reciting a mantra you simply listen to the sound. The "awareness part of practice" is to listen to the sound and keep it as the focus of your attention without straying so that you ignore wandering thoughts when they arise. Sometimes a prayer, because of the sounds, is also a mantra such as the *"La ilaha ill-Allah"* recited everyday within Islam.

Mantras are usually constructed of special syllables, particularly the "Ah" or "Ohm" sounds, that help improve the energy flow within your body and help your mind to become quiet and relaxed. As you recite these special sounds it helps to temper your breathing, and one of the tricks to mantra practice to develop a rhythm of recitation that matches with your breathing. That's how you produce the most powerful effects of mental quieting and harmonious body feelings at the same time.

Some people say that mantra recitation changes the vibrational frequency of your body and mind, but what they actually mean is that it changes the rhythm of the energy flow within your body that is called "*chi*" in China or "*prana*" in India. When this *chi* flow becomes more calm and peaceful because you have used mantra recitation as a sort of "sound yoga" to make it more rhythmical and regular, your mind will quiet because of a linkage between your internal vital energy and your thoughts. Your thoughts "ride" on this energy (are connected with it), so if you can calm this internal energy then you can calm your mind.

There is a very large science behind the construction of mantras because of what the specific root sounds (*bijas*) and order of the sounds can do to calm your mind and adjust your internal energy flow, but you don't need to know any of this. Sounds are non-denominational, so you simply want to use the results of this science and the recitation of certain sounds to get the results of mental quieting you are after. Because you listen to the sounds of the mantra while ignoring all other wandering thoughts, your unwavering concentration causes wandering thoughts in your mind to eventually die down so that your mind becomes quiet. In short, reciting mantras is calming and you don't need to know the exact science as to why they work because nothing evil or nefarious is going on.

There are many mantras or prayers you can use in mantra recitation practice, but it is best to use the ones that have been proven over the millennia to produce excellent results. These are typically the most popular mantras, and they are popular because they are proven to work at mental calming. You can go to the internet and readily find famous mantras such as the following:

- Ani Yod Heh Vav Heh (Judaism)
- La Ilaha Ill-Allah (Islam)
- Ma-Ra-Na-Tha (Christianity)
- Ohm Mani Padme Hum (Buddhism)
- Ohm Namo Shivaya (Hinduism)

The mantra I most often recommend for recitation is the Zhunti mantra, which runs as follows: "Namo saptanam samyaksambuddha kotinam tadyatha om cale cule cundhi svaha." This mantra is said to help calm your mind, change your fortune so you can achieve whatever you want, and help open up your energy channels so that you can attain all the blessings meditation can possibly bring.

To practice any mantra you simply recite the phrase over and over again, and while doing so you should just listen to the sounds, while ignoring everything else. This act of concentration will then tie up all your wandering thoughts. When you find your mind straying while reciting mantras, just bring the focus of your mind back to listening to the mantra sounds once again. That's all you have to do. The practice is as simple as that.

By listening to the sounds of the mantra you will tie up your thinking consciousness, and then the wandering thoughts inside your mind will die down so that you eventually experience a peaceful inner state of mind. As you recite a mantra your breathing will become more rhythmical, your breathing will calm down, your respiration will soften, and your mind will become more quiet. You just listen to the sounds you are reciting and your mind, your internal energy (*chi*), and body will eventually all become unified together so that they move and rest together. If your breathing or mind ever halt during mantra practice, you simply stop and stay in that state of cessation for as long as possible. At that time we say that your mind and *chi* have become one because both will have reached a stage of "emptiness," "quiet," "halting" or "cessation."

Now you know that the basic purpose of mantra recitation practice is to tie up the wandering mind of your busy consciousness through the practice of listening. You want to use the fact that you are concentrating on listening to a set of sounds to tie up all the other thoughts running around in your head and thereby produce internal peace and quiet. Mantra recitation is just that simple. It is nothing mysterious. By listening to something with concentration, you ignore everything else and thus those thoughts die down. By reciting certain sounds, it also helps change your internal energy flow, which in turn helps your body and mind achieve a higher stage of purity. This is why the mantra you use is important.

Basically, mantra recitation helps you get rid of the excessive internal thought chatter you always hear in your head so that your mind becomes empty, clear and bright. This state of cessation produces an empty mind, as do all meditation practices, and because it seems empty it is also called a "mind of purity." A "mind of purity" doesn't mean you are more virtuous, but simply means that there are less thoughts running about because they have emptied out.

You can make mantras far more powerful and effective by matching their natural recitation rhythm with the rhythms of your breathing, and then they will start to affect the flow of vital energy within your body. As stated, by linking up with the feeling of that rhythmical energy inside you it is said that your mind, your breathing and energy can all become unified as one. This is when mantra recitation becomes *mantrayoga* practice. The "ma" within "*mantrayoga*" stands for the mind while "tra" stands for *chi* (*prana*) so *mantrayoga* means unifying your mind with your *chi*. Your mind and your *chi* will always become unified if you practice mantras correctly, and this is the whole point of practice. Your mantra (or prayer) recitation should follow a very natural rhythm if you want to accomplish this.

Only advanced practitioners who practice listening without attachment to thoughts can achieve this unity, and many schools encourage practitioners to try to attain this. For instance, in Islam the recitation of mantras in conjunction with your breathing is a practice called "*dhikr.*" In Orthodox Christianity, practitioners recite the Prayer of the Heart along with special breathing rhythms (and often visualization exercises) to produce a stilling of the mind. In

Tibetan Buddhism, the practitioners recite mantras in conjunction with performing visualization practices at the same time, too. These are just a few examples of the many spiritual traditions which use mantras to adjust your internal energies and achieve quiet states of mind.

After you arrive at a state where thoughts have calmed down (cessation) because of mantra practice, then you can rest in and enjoy the state of mental cessation (quiet mind) you have reached. At that point you should rest in emptiness and observe that quiet state to contemplate the nature of your mind. You don't have to continue reciting mantras once you reach this state of cessation, but just stay in that quiet and observe the fact that consciousness is empty. Quiet is the mind's natural state, but few people realize this because they are always attaching to the thoughts which make their minds busy. Once you realize that the natural state of consciousness is empty, it becomes easier to let go of wandering thoughts and cultivate a higher degree of mental clarity and internal calmness.

There are three typical styles of mantra recitation you should know about. You can chant a mantra out loud, where everyone can hear you, and you can do this by yourself at home or in a group practice session with others.

The second method is to recite a mantra with your mouth half open or lips nearly closed so that the mantra is barely audible to others. You are not reciting the mantra solely in your mind, and yet it is inaudible to others. This is also done in conjunction with the rhythm of your breathing and internal energy.

The last method is to mentally chant the mantra within

your mind so no one can hear what you are doing, and this is the most common and powerful method you should learn.

Many people set themselves a certain target for the number of mantras they wish to recite per day, and we encourage this practice wholeheartedly. Until it became a habit, I had a certain target number of repetitions I always tried to recite each day and recorded my progress each night before sleeping. If I could not complete that number of repetitions, then I would work harder to make up the deficiency the very next day. By scheduling the daily number of mantra repetitions I was to perform, I made a lot of progress in meditation practice this way.

When you recite a mantra, you should try to do so in conjunction with smooth, rhythmical breathing that suits the sound. After a long time in doing so, your belly may become warm, which means your energy channels are opening up in that region, and your breathing may even slow down or stop. If that happens, you should stay in that state of cessation. You should rest in that state without forcing yourself to begin reciting mantras again and just let their return come naturally.

That quiet restful state is what you are trying to reach, not the continuance of the mantra. In other words, the purpose of mantra recitation is to help you reach a state where your breathing slows, your mind quiets and your internal energy rises. Your purpose should not be to recite a certain number of mantras per day, but to recite an amount sufficient to reach this state, which is the true objective of practice.

If ever you reach this state during a practice session, then even if you are in a group with others reciting mantras or have not recited your targeted number of repetitions, stop reciting and just remain in that peacefulness while your internal energy arises and starts to open up your acupuncture meridians. In other words, once you reach some state of cessation, forget about everything else and just stay in that state of emptiness. This is achieving the intended results of practice. *Forget about the mantra when this happens and stay in the state of cessation!*

Mantras have many purposes. Some mantras have meanings that request protection from higher powers or assistance so that you can accomplish certain deeds in the world. The more powerful ones with sacred lineages tap into the power of enlightened beings who have vowed to help individuals attain enlightenment.

You can even use mantras to adjust the internal energy flow within your body, such as trying to help open regions where there are many energy channels. When you use mantras attached to (as if from) certain parts of the body, this advanced type of practice becomes *mantrayoga* (mantra yoga). This is a special type of internal energy work using sound to help open up the *chi* channels in those areas for health or spiritual purposes.

Regardless as to why you want to use mantras, the point of mantra recitation is to help you calm your mind through sound and when you finally reach that state of calming where even the body reduces its coarse breathing, you must try to stay in that state and enjoy it. Then you will achieve the results of practice. At that time your internal energy will be pushing through all your acupuncture meridians to clear them out, and this is an excellent sign of progress.

6
VISUALIZATION PRACTICE

Another popular meditation technique for busy minds is visualization practice. You should consider visualization practice a special type of "concentration practice" which uses mental images you construct yourself. The basic method of visualization practice is that you form some particular image in your mind and then practice holding that mental image with stability.

If you can hold a mental image with stability, this certainly means you have gotten rid of some degree of distracting random thoughts, otherwise you would never be able to accomplish this feat in the first place. If you can get rid of wandering thoughts then you can enjoy some of the peace and purity promised by meditation, so you first practice holding onto some mental image, and when you achieve success in attaining lucid stability of that internal picture, you let go of that image and rest in mental emptiness, or cessation.

You can, for instance, look at some external object and try to memorize that image. You stabilize your concentration on that object until you can see it internally while your eyes are closed or when you are not looking at the object. Next, you take that mental image as your new object, and then stabilize your internal attention on it, visualizing it with as much detail as possible, until your concentration is unwavering.

Once that internal picture is stable, you can let go of the image to experience a peaceful mind that is relatively empty. Thus, you are using the practice of concentration on a visual image to banish wandering thoughts, rather than listen to a sound as is done with mantras, and when they are gone, you let go of the image you are holding onto so that you can experience a mind that is peaceful.

That's it. That's the entire practice. There is nothing mysterious, supernatural or even complicated about visualization practice. You can choose to concentrate on forming an image of a very complicated picture, but that still doesn't make the practice in any way supernatural or mysterious. That just makes it more difficult to do, that's all.

Visualization practice is excellent mental training. It involves training yourself to concentrate for a long period of time, so through it you can learn how to hold your mind with one-pointed concentration. With mantra practice you listen to internal sounds to calm your mind, but with visualization practice you look at internal images to try and calm your mind of random thoughts. In both cases you use concentration to ignore, or we can say "tie up," wandering thoughts. That's what produces mental quiet.

Various spiritual traditions propose a variety of different images you might visualize within your mind. Tibetan Buddhism, for instance, specializes in this type of mental training using complicated images. Some yoga traditions ask you to visualize with stability the simple image of a circle that is yellow, blue, red, white or some other color. Some spiritual traditions suggest you envision an image of an enlightened individual's face. In Taoism practitioners often visualize the layout of the stars in the Big Dipper.

There have been all sorts of images proposed as items for mental concentration, and for starting out simplest is best. None of these images are "holy" in themselves. They are just better or worse images for concentration practice, and whether they are better or worse all depends on the individual. If one type of image used in practice helps you calm your mind, then it is a good one. If it doesn't, then why use the one which is less effective?

In some cases, you can even put your practice efforts into learning how to form stable mental pictures of things that are moving, such as a waterwheel or the linked gears within a clock. This is how many scientists and inventors trained their minds in the past, and many attributed their great creativity to the powers of visualization they practiced and developed. We always encourage scientists, mathematicians and even athletes to learn visualization practice starting from when they are young.

The point of visualization practice is that you want to train your mind to be able to focus on holding some simple internal image, and you want to learn to hold that image with stability. You can only hold an image without losing it if you develop concentration, so this type of meditation method is described as a way of cultivating one-pointed concentration. Basically, it builds your concentration muscles. There is certainly nothing wrong with that!

In order to focus with concentration, you must earn how to ignore the distraction of wandering thoughts that plague your mind, which is the goal of meditation, and after you do this you can let go of the image and enjoy a peaceful, empty mind. When you practice visualization exercises, your one-pointedness of concentration on holding your mental image settles your wandering thoughts, and that resultantly produces mental clearness and calmness. Visualization exercises are therefore good for teaching concentration because visualization is a skill that will serve you well in life.

Some people are especially gifted with natural powers of concentration, but many of cannot concentrate at all. Thus visualization practices are the type of exercise some people will often find the most helpful even though they are the most troublesome. People with busy minds can practice visualization exercises as a way to cultivate steady concentration, and then afterwards let go of their imagined image to experience some degree of mental emptiness after their minds have stopped wandering. In other words, once you reach a quiet mind, that means that your thoughts have calmed down and that the mental emptiness is stable, so stop practicing. At that point, you should switch to resting in that emptiness where you can observe (or contemplate) the empty quiet nature of your mind. Once you reach some degree of emptiness, just rest in the emptiness while staying aware rather than falling asleep. Just let go of everything—everything you define as consciousness—and then your internal energies will arise, your breathing will slow, and you will enter into an even deeper mental peace.

One of the most popular visualization exercises along these lines comes to us from ancient India, and is called the "White Skeleton Visualization" practice. It is very powerful because it helps you cultivate stable concentration to attain mental quieting, and it helps to cultivate your internal energy at the same time. The basic practice method is as follows.

First, find a quiet place to sit, preferably in the lotus posture (although you can even do this method when you are sitting on a chair or couch). Now focus your attention on the big toe of your left foot. You always start this visualization practice with your *left big toe!* This is a very important instruction. You can even try to feel the inside of the toe if you wish, but that is not necessary for this practice. In fact, the ability to "feel" the energy currents running along your bones only comes after a high stage of practice effort.

Once your attention is initially fixed on your left big toe, imagine that a blister forms and that the skin peels away to reveal the bone underneath. Now imagine that this toe bone becomes shining white in color. For this meditation, you will always progressively imagine stripping off the flesh from the bones, working from below going upwards to reveal the bones underneath, but whenever you imagine the bones you must visualize them as white in color and shining brightly. Thus this visualization method is often called the dazzling white skeleton visualization technique.

Once you can see the white big toe in your mind's eye, next observe two or three toes. See, within your mind's eye, the white bones within your toes shining brightly. Gradually extend the image of the toes on the left foot until you can visualize all five shining brightly with white light.

You want to try to clearly discern the bones, which is why many people buy an anatomy book or small skeleton to help master this visualization practice. You want to see them as clearly distinguishable as possible and the color of dazzling white snow. Your task is to fix your attention on creating a stable image of the five bright white toes without straying. If you lose your attention, you can start from the beginning or begin again where you left off. The rule is that when you lose focus or your mind wanders, just return to your meditation practice once again.

As you begin to master this visualization, you might feel a warm energy or pulsation in the areas you concentrate upon. You might even have dreams about the color of your skeleton or the energy pathways within your body. This is because your vital energy becomes activated in those areas and starts to open up the energy channels in those regions. While it is difficult to open up the energy meridians in your hands *and particularly the feet* (which is why you start with the toes), you must be sure not to neglect the areas of the knee caps, shoulders and skull which contain bundles of countless *chi* routes that must become clearly defined and differentiated.

Because it is most difficult to open up the channels in the feet, this is why we always start by visualizing them first with this practice, and we always initially focus on the left big toe. Then we progressively visualize stripping off the flesh and revealing the bones in the left foot, then right foot, then left leg bones (fibula and tibia), then right leg bones, then the knee caps, femurs, pelvis and spine. We always work our way upwards starting with the left side, which stands for the *chi* or energy of the body.

Each new set of bones is visualized after the flesh is imagined as falling away. When we get to the shoulders we must pay special attention to visualize those bones correctly and then the bones from the shoulder to the elbow, then from the elbow to the wrist, next to the hand bones and so forth. Each time we want to visualize the bones, we first imagine the flesh splitting open or falling away so that only the shining white bones are left. Sometimes you can even try to feel the *chi* (energy) of the bones within your body, but you must not get attached to any of these feelings. That type of internal energy work is a totally different type of cultivation practice.

Finally after going through all your bones, you will be able to visualize a complete dazzling white skeleton. When you can do that, or even if the picture is incomplete, you should hold that image for awhile with some stability and then release it to experience an empty mind that is relatively free of random thoughts and distractions.

To perform the release of the image, just imagine that your entire skeleton then turns to dust that is blown away, and the only thing left is then vast empty space. Just rest your mind in the image of that empty space and totally let go. All the energy within your body will become harmonized through this technique, and distracting thoughts dissolved away, so when you release your visualized image you can then rest in experiencing a mental emptiness like space.

There are actually over thirty different versions of this basic white skeleton visualization practice, and you must pick a version that works for you. Sometimes you can practice several versions simultaneously, and you can change the method based on your body situation and circumstances.

Some versions were developed for specific purposes, such as for high blood pressure. In that technique, you first imagine your body becoming a white skeleton and that your skull becomes detached and is placed lying on your lap but flipped upside down. You can also imagine that all your white toe bones become little candle flames to help reduce high blood pressure as well.

Another white skeleton method has you imagine that your skeleton descends into your hollow abdomen where it dissolves into a bright white light. You hold onto the image of that light within your abdomen until it dissipates and you just experience empty space once again.

Other methods have you concentrate on visualizing specific areas of the body, after all the flesh has been removed and your body has become only white bones in that section, to help assist in reducing pain (such as for arthritis) and curing specific syndromes or diseases. For cancer, practitioners are often taught to visualize that their entire body of flesh burns with fire and then turns into the white bones, which are burning as well. Then those shiny white bones turn into dust that is once again blown away to leave you with mental peace, emptiness or quiet. Afterwards, the practitioner rests their mind in that state of mental emptiness.

The white skeleton visualization practice is one of the special meditation methods that helps you heal your body and purify its internal energies. It contributes to improving your health and longevity while also serving as a means of mental calming and spiritual practice. There is nothing mysterious about it, for its principles have already been explained. The only warning is that it should not be practiced by people with strong sexual desires because those sexual desires will tend to increase when the vital energy arises from using this technique. People with strong sexual desires should usually practice breathing methods for their cultivation because they can use various breathing techniques to help smoothen and harmonize the internal energies within their body. If stronger sexual desires arise from using this technique, then you can try to manage them through the diet, exercise and through breathing practices.

People who have strong sexual desires tend to be healthy and can use that strong energy to succeed in cultivation if they meditate, but they need to learn how to channel that energy by adjusting the body through diet, breathing and exercise so they don't lose those pushing energies. Those energies are valuable for opening up your *chi* channels, so you don't want to lose them carelessly. This is why many spiritual traditions tell people to retain them.

You should know that the traditional ways to adjust sexual desire, so that you don't lose those energies through sexual activities (and their retention is then channeled to working on opening up your internal energy meridians), are by decreasing your food intake, by imagining the energy in your body rises out the top of your head (while you forget your body and mind), through breathing practices (including mantra and prayer recitation since they move internal energies) and through exercise. Another method to prevent the loss of those energies is to practice sexual relations without ejaculation, which is a type of sexual yoga.

None of these methods or results are religious. They are just various ways to adjust your body. People who cultivate meditation or other practices should not use the name of religion for their efforts but just apply these non-denominational methods to help improve their lives, and then they will really become able to prove something transcendental that is a real accomplishment for their life. Cultivation is a kind of science, the science of human development, and we simply use this science in our efforts at self-improvement.

7
ANAPANA PRACTICE

One of the most recommended meditation methods is for practitioners to concentrate on watching their breathing because, like the skeleton visualization method, this practice also helps transform both your body and mind. The highest method for doing this is called *anapana* practice.

Anapana practice, which entails watching your breath (and then later observing the sensations of internal energy in your body), is based on the principle that your breathing and your internal energy (*chi*) are linked, and that your breathing and energy also affect your consciousness (your thoughts). Your thoughts and breathing certainly move in tandem, and you can use your breathing to help control your mind or vice versa. You can also use your breathing to affect your internal energy, which yoga calls "igniting" it, and the movements of this energy are also connected to your consciousness.

You probably already know from personal life experience that if your mind calms down then your breathing will calm down, and your internal energy circulation will also become smoother and more regular. We call that natural result "feeling balanced" or "feeling harmonious."

You can read many old books on meditation topics that use pretty phrases like this, but they always refer to very common results that we have all touched in our lives, such as when we are feeling rather comfortable and balanced. However, people who read these phrases from ancient books typically think they are speaking of ephemeral mystical states when they are always speaking of something very ordinary, and yet hard to achieve on a regular basis in daily life unless we make specific efforts to cultivate it so that it becomes more common.

If your breathing calms down then your internal energy circulation will become more regular and peaceful, and your mind will similarly become calm and empty of wandering thoughts because of the interconnection between your body and mind. You can use a softening of your breathing to calm your mind, or can use meditation to calm down your mind and thereby calm your breathing. Both of these avenues, of breathing or thoughts, can be used to adjust your internal energy. In life we must always learn ways to adjust our bodies and minds, and one of the secrets is that we can certainly do so through our breathing, but hardly anyone ever teaches this except in yoga and martial arts.

The main meditation practice of cultivating your breathing,

anapana, comes from Buddhism and is different from but similar to the *pranayama* breathing practices found within Indian yoga. Various techniques where you cultivate your breathing are also very popular in Chinese Taoism, Sufism, the Eastern Orthodox Christian Church and many other spiritual traditions.

The basis of many unusual cultivation techniques within Tibetan Esoteric Buddhism, and many *nei-gong* internal martial arts practices, is also the idea of cultivating your breathing and using that leveraging mechanism to adjust the internal *chi* of your body. This is also the basis of many internal energy practices found in the schools of yoga, *qi-gong*, and *kundalini* cultivation. People think these practices are mysterious, but they are all dependent on simple proven relationships between your breathing, your *chi*, and your consciousness.

Most of these meditation schools, even the esoteric traditions, tell practitioners to focus on their breathing until it calms down, and then your mind will become quiet. You focus your attention on your breathing and observe it without interfering with its motions. You watch your own breathing, without interference, just as if you were watching a sleeping baby and its inhalations and exhalations. You don't cling to your respiratory process or try to move it or push it in any way while you are watching it, but just watch it. You just know it. You just put your attention solely on this and observe it while ignoring other distractions. You are aware of the sensations within your body, but don't attach to them either.

As you progress with this practice, you will eventually

71

become more fully aware of all the sensations of energy movements inside your body, but you should not attach to them or get entangled in them just like you should not attach to your thoughts when doing any other forms of meditation practice. You just watch or know all these things with detachment. In this case your attention remains on feeling internal energy movements, but you must not cling to these types of feelings.

The basis of *anapana* meditation practice is as follows. In most other types of meditation practice you simply watch your thoughts without attaching to them and then in time they will calm down. This is a rule of nature so it always happens. If you tie up your wandering thoughts by concentrating on a sound or mental image, thoughts will calm down through these avenues as well.

In *anapana* practice, you focus on staying aware of a specific type of thought, and once again this is the practice of concentration because it requires that you ignore everything else and just stay focused on this as the object of your attention. When your attention is focused on one place or spot, that's concentration. When it is really focused tightly that is one-pointed concentration, which then ties up thoughts and produces quiet stability.

Therefore with *anapana* you concentrate on observing the feelings of your breathing and internal energies inside your body. You notice those sensations, but you don't become attached to them. You stay independent of them and never lose your presence of mind. You stay centered and always know what is happening within your consciousness. You know the energy is moving here or there, or feels hot or cold inside you, but you don't attach to those feelings. You just know them because this is where you are shining your awareness, and you ignore everything else except this target of observation. Sometimes you can feel the entire energy of the body, so you stay aware of that feeling without clinging to it or forcing it to do anything.

Naturally you cannot sense any internal energies right away from doing this practice because people normally cannot feel anything inside them at all until their energy channels start to open. Therefore you first start by observing your respiration until it calms. If you do this correctly while not attaching to it, you can reach a point of "respiratory cessation" that will enhance the development of *chi* energy within your body. Then you will start to feel the internal energy of your body when it becomes activated, but it is hard to reach this stage of activation since it takes a lot of practice effort. Therefore the method of watching your breathing should eventually morph into a method of observing your internal energy once you can feel it. It takes diligent practice over time to get to a high enough stage of practice where feeling your internal *chi* energy becomes possible.

In watching your breathing and internal energies without interference—by focusing on just watching your inhalation and exhalation process to the exclusion of everything else—you establish a point of focus for your mind that forces you to ignore wandering thoughts. That's what you did in the other types of meditation practice we covered. Your physical sensations, rather than sounds or mental images, will now serve as the focal point for your concentration.

As with these other meditation practices, when you start thinking of something else while doing *anapana* practice, it means your mind is straying and you should just return to watching your breathing once again, and try to actually feel the breath or energy inside you.

Because it is difficult for some people to remain concentrated on their breathing (because they end up following other wandering thoughts), some cultivation schools have developed concentration methods where they want you to count your breaths so you stay focused on the breathing. This can help some people learn how to concentrate, but the strategy of counting should only be used by beginners, if at all. It is not something you necessarily need to do, and not something you must always use.

The general rules are that if you eat too much, have high blood pressure, cannot sleep or have lots of miscellaneous thoughts and desires, you should count the out-breaths of your breathing. If your body has a weak or feeble constitution or you have low blood pressure, then you typically count your in-breaths. If your body is neither in particularly great shape or bad shape, the general rule is to count your out-breaths before noon and in-breaths after noon. You simply count your respirations from one to ten, and then start over again.

When from this practice you start to be aware of the pause in-between each breath, *anapana* practice then enters the stage of "following the breath" throughout the body. Counting should then be abandoned and you should start focusing on the state of respiratory pausation, or cessation, that is in-between your inhalations and exhalations.

The arithmetic of the counting is not the important thing with this practice. The important thing is to try to stay focused on your breathing, without adding energy to it, and learning to let go of your respiratory process so that it can settle. Then you particularly focus on the gap between inhalations or exhalations, and try to gently extend the amount of time you stay in that state of cessation. The counting is not the important thing. The period of respiratory cessation is the important thing!

People who count their breaths usually don't know that lengthening the gap between the in-breaths and out-breaths is the important thing, but this is what *anapana* practice is all about. The counting is only used to help you initially stay focused on watching your breath, instead of following other wandering thoughts, until your breathing calms down. It is just used to help you maintain your focus and concentration until you reach a state of respiratory stopping that we have always called "cessation." In yoga this is called the stage of natural "*kumbhaka*." If you don't need any counting to stay focused and concentrated on following your breathing, then you certainly should not complicate matters and use it. Whatever methods you use, the state of respiratory cessation you reach is the important thing because it leads to the next stage of practice.

Anapana practice often seems initially hard for most people because the human mind likes to wander. It has a hard time staying concentrated on anything, even a simple task such as watching the breathing. This is why we want to learn meditation because if we can reduce our tendency to follow wandering thoughts, our minds will become clearer and more peaceful. Our ability to concentrate for long periods of time, on any topic, will also improve. Improving our concentration skills is extremely important in this age of short attention spans and endless distractions. Hence, don't give up with your efforts at mastering *anapana* practice because you initially think it is difficult and that you won't be able to do it. You can certainly master any skill through discipline and diligent practice over time. *Anapana* practice follows this rule of mastery just like anything else.

Eventually over time your breathing will eventually calm down and then your thoughts will calm down. This is like hitting two birds with one stone. When your respiration and thoughts both calm down, then your internal energy will truly start to arise within your body. This is a principle of human physiology that most people don't know because they never practice meditation, but once again it is a result common to the human organism. No matter how old you are and regardless of race, gender, religion, education, nationality or any other division, these are rules of the human organism and human nature.

When your breathing slows to a halt and your mind becomes relatively quiet and empty at the same time, that is the first major target for this type of meditation practice. During that state of cessation (where thoughts and breathing have calmed down, so we say they have "ceased"), your internal energies will then start to open up your acupuncture energy meridians (*chi* channels) which will in turn eventually lead to an even deeper calming of your mind. You are becoming healthier inside and mentally more calm and quiet.

This meditation practice will quickly improve your mental clarity and alertness, and it enhances your overall health and brain function in general. It has been used by many great literary figures throughout history, such as poets and writers, and by those who wish to cultivate the internal energies of their bodies. It leads to a special clarity and calmness of the mind, especially when combined with various *pranayama* practices from India that teach you how to hold your breath. Those methods can help you quickly master and further develop upon this basic process. The big take-away principle is that if you really want sharper focus, a brighter mind, and more mental acuity, you should practice some form of breathing practices on a daily basis. This will result in fewer sicknesses during your life and a longer life span as well.

The fundamental idea of reaching a state where your external respiration ceases, but the internal energy within you then arises and starts to take over, is the foundational practice that is the basis of many *nei-gong* internal energy methods in the martial arts, Taoism, Buddhism, and yoga. The idea is so simple, and yet few people ever practice correctly or long enough to reach this stage, so most human beings don't even know that it exits. It cannot be achieved in one day because you need plenty of prior practice effort to open enough *chi* channels within your body so that your internal energies will arise when your respiration slows.

In other words, it takes time, discipline, patience and consistent practice to achieve this, yet this is the basis of better health and longevity. Only if you open up your internal *chi* channels can you banish latent sicknesses and illnesses from your body, eliminate poisons and impurities, and create the foundation for a longer and healthier life. The purification of your energy channels can bring about a disease-free body, and so health and longevity can be attained by practicing breathing methods.

In many ancient yoga texts it is said that only *pranayama* is necessary to purify your body, but the meaning is that your *chi* must become activated inside your body to totally open your energy channels, and you can activate it through *pranayama*. You must use *pranayama* to reach a stage of inner *nei-gong* practice that entails internal energy work beyond external respiratory practices. *Anapana* leads to this superior stage of practice, and results in some degree of "energy channel detoxification" that cannot be achieved through any other means. This is the meaning of physical body purification through *pranayama* or *anapana*.

In any case, the basic technique to practice is that you sit there in a meditation posture and become aware of every movement of your breathing until it starts to calm down and almost stops. That can only happen if you let go of your body. Your body is not the "real you" but just something which *appears within your consciousness*, so let go of your mind and body and see what happens. Your breathing will still function on its own, so just let go of it and see what happens as it calms down and settles.

Sometimes this calming of your breathing will happen naturally from prolonged mantra practice. Sometimes it will happen just from watching your thoughts. Sometimes it will happen because you are concentrating on forming internal visualizations and ignoring everything else. If you become really absorbed with visualization practice, then at that time you will be ignoring all wandering thoughts, so your breathing will resultantly calm down. Mantra practice, just by itself, will also help regulate the *chi* of your body so that it becomes smooth and harmonious, and then your breathing will also calm down through this vehicle as well. All these methods of meditation lead to the same end result, but it is most clearly delineated with *anapana* practice.

The possible effectiveness of mantras in achieving this result is why we always recommend you use the mantras proven to accomplish this rather than recite affirmations or prayers someone has created without regards to mantra science. They cannot possibly achieve the same internal energy effects. Accordingly, the mantras of Buddhism and Hinduism are best along these lines for helping to transform your *chi* channels and harmonize the *chi* flow within your body. In any case, many cultivation practices can help you temper and harmonize your breathing and the internal energies within your body just as the singing of Gregorian chants in Latin helps Christian monks accomplish the same feat.

Hence, the calming of your respiration doesn't have to happen through the route of practicing *anapana*, but it is easiest to produce this result from the meditation practice of watching your breath. When it calms down you have accomplished the first part of the practice. Once your breathing starts slowing down and then stops because you no longer attach to it, you can try to hold onto that state of respiratory cessation with the tiniest bit of pressure so that your internal energies are encouraged to open up more *chi* channels inside.

Once your breath calms down to a state of cessation, you should definitely focus on the empty, non-moving state of pausation between the in-breaths and the out-breaths. This stationary gap of resting is the most important part of the practice. This is a point of respiratory stopping or cessation, and your mind will be quiet at that time. Because your mind will be quieter, it is also called a state of mental cessation (though of course there will still be thoughts in your head). If your mind had not become calm then your breathing could not have calmed down either.

Here is the key thing to do at this point: when your breathing slows to a halt, you should focus on that interval between your respirations (after an exhalation) until a state of internal breathing takes over. You will start to feel this internal energy, such as a warmness or pumping sensation in the lower belly, and then you should also just observe whatever happens. Always just observe, watch, witness, or know what is going on but don't interfere with it. It is impossible to harm your body or mind in any way with this or any other meditation practice, so just let go of your entire body and its breathing process, stop holding onto your thoughts, and see what happens. You are simply resting your body and mind, so what possible harm can befall you? Nothing at all! Your body knows what it is doing in opening up all its energy channels, so don't interfere with it.

Once your breathing slows down and then stops, your

consciousness can connect with your internal vital energy, or *chi* (*prana*), through attention. However, as long as your breathing is scattered or keeps flowing in and out, your wandering thoughts will keep coming and going and you will never reach this state of physical transformation.

In *anapana* practice, you simply know the movements of your *chi* through awareness and observation of inner sensations. You observe your breathing until it calms down, and with enough practice your internal *chi* energy will start to become activated. Breathing and mind calm down until they unite of themselves, and then your internal energy becomes activated. You will feel these sensations, and you still just observe them. You then switch from focusing on your external breathing to knowing the doings of all the *chi* within your body. A very high stage practitioner can feel all the *chi* within their body as one entire unit, or feel streams of energy moving here and there, but this requires quite a lot of *anapana* practice.

It is just a fact that when your external breathing naturally subsides from calming, at that point your body will start generating its own inner *chi* energy. This is the real *chi* of your body, and when it arises it is technically called the awakening or arousal of *kundalini*. In other words, when your external breathing subsides into a period of pausation, the inner energy flow of your body becomes activated and starts clearing out all your energy meridians. Whether it happens slowly or fast, whether the feeling is very subtle or pronounced, this constitutes a *kundalini* awakening.

By ignoring everything else in the world but just watching

your breathing, your breathing will become so light that the flow of air from respiration will spontaneously stop, and the body will then open up its energy channels to come alive with its own inner life-breath. This is a law of the human organism, and is the actual objective of the yoga schools, Taoism, Buddhism, Hinduism, and the martial arts.

When the body switches to this inner respiration, it produces its own vital energy without relying on external respiration. Your body-mind then starts to become rejuvenated because it begins to generate energy by itself, and your brain and all other cells will then start to fill with this pure life-energy. This is why the body becomes warm, light, supple, and softens from meditation practice, and why people who meditate recover their health and extend their life-span. Through meditation you can even banish depression because you increase or recover lost internal energy and vigor.

Because the mind is quiet at this stage and your breathing has stopped, too, ancient schools poetically say that mind and breath have "become one" or both have "become empty." In these ancient sayings, the word "breath" actually refers to the *chi* energy inside you rather than your respiration. You use the practice of following your external breathing to ignite the internal *chi* energy inside you and set it into motion. Then you put your attention on the *chi*. The fact that your attention is now focused on your *chi* means that you have unified the two because your mind isn't focused elsewhere. Your energy arises and your mind is focused on it, so they are unified together. You are aware of your *chi*, so "the two have become one." Once that internal energy set into motion, you are accomplishing the entire purpose of this practice.

The ancient saying, "when the mind and the inner breath (*chi* energy) become one, both air and thoughts stop coming and going," explains this entire process. This basically means that the external process of air-breathing subsides while the mind simultaneously quiets, and then the real internal energy of the body starts arising. Then you focus on that, which is the point of practice. Focusing on your breathing is just used to get you to this stage just as reciting and listening to mantras is used to lead you to a state where your breathing and mind both settle. You use the *anapana* practice of watching your breath to get to this stage of cultivating your internal energy, and that energy will transform your body so that you enter a deeper stage of meditation. You use this method as you would use a match to light a fire, and after the fire is lit (after the internal energy is activated and starts moving), you don't need the match anymore.

For instance, here is another simple method some people may want to try after they develop a lot of experience with *anapana*. After you have been meditating for awhile and reach a state of mental calmness, when you exhale your breath from within a state of respiratory calmness, don't breathe in again. Just hold that state of breathlessness (empty lungs) after exhalation, but use the slightest amount of pressure to do so. Don't use any force in doing so. At the same time, let go of your body and forget about all your senses of hearing, feeling, seeing, etc. Ignore all your senses and body sensations, and just focus on the top of your nose between your eyebrows while your mind is relatively empty and quiet.

When you first start to practice this, it may initially seem difficult but will get easier as time goes by. This meditation method to help you let go of your body while your real *chi* (internal energy) rises so that you can train to enter into a deeper meditation state. *Anapana* is just one of the many cultivation methods based on the connection between breathing, internal *chi* energy and consciousness. This particular method helps encourage your internal energy to help open up your *chi* channels.

In *anapana* practice you must activate and then directly experience your internal *chi* energy, and only then is it considered real *anapana* practice. You are stopping your breath through deliberate actions for the sake of igniting this *chi* energy, and you want to ignite this *chi* energy for the sake of transforming your body. Only if your body becomes transformed will you be able to achieve the highest results of meditation practice.

With *anapana*, you watch (observe) the doings of the internal energies of your body. You first start by observing your respiration, and then the *chi* energies of your body when they start arising. You cannot open your *chi* channels using your mind. You cannot open them using any type of force or visualization. Only your internal energies can themselves open up your *chi* channels. Hence with *anapana*, you simply observe those energies in a detached manner, as a third person observer would, and then those energies will then become free to open up all sorts of internal *chi* circulations. As your *chi* routes become opened and your internal *chi* circulation becomes better, your mind will calm down and become emptier due to this progress. Hence you will get all sorts of physical and mental benefits from this practice.

8
SETTING UP A
PRACTICE SCHEDULE

You can only make progress with meditation when you practice on a regular basis. The key to mastering any skill, whether it be yoga or martial arts or even ice skating, is to practice that skill consistently over time. In order to learn how to meditate, you must certainly follow this principle of consistent practice as well.

The problem is that we all have busy lives, so how can we spare the time for regular meditation practice? How can we become diligent about it?

The answer is that you must schedule your meditation practice to fit it into your life, and record your progress. We respect whatever we measure, and measurement ends argument, so by scheduling your efforts and keeping a track record of your efforts so you can see if you are following through with the commitment you want to make. You must make meditation part of your daily routine, and to do that you must schedule it into your life. As to what time is best, this is entirely up to you, but you must schedule that commitment.

You can meditate anytime you want, but it is traditionally said that four times are considered the best: predawn, morning, afternoon, and at nightfall. In the yoga schools that teach *pranayama*, they tell you to practice four times per day as well. But forget that. You basically want to practice whenever you can fit it into your schedule, but you want to avoid meditating immediately after eating because that will tend to make you sleepy.

An common amount of time for meditation practice is at least a 20-30 minute session, and then practitioners often stop or take a break. Once you can meditate for this amount of time you can gradually build up to a longer session period. Even 15-20 minutes is fine as long as you start the habit of daily meditation practice. There is actually no perfect amount of practice time such as a 20, 30, or 40 minute meditation session. There is only the time you can spare for meditation, and you need at least 15-20 minutes to get started.

Since there is no perfect time to meditate, some people practice when they wake up in the morning, some late at night, and some before meals. Everyone is different because bodies are different, circumstances are different and schedules are different. Whatever you can spare to get started is the right amount of time, and whenever you can practice to get started is the right time to practice. No conditions are ever perfect, so the key principle is to just get started. Don't make anything a barrier to getting started, including the cross-legged lotus sitting posture. If it turns out you don't want to practice because sitting with crossed legs is uncomfortable, then use some other position to get started. Once you establish the habit of meditation practice, then you can get back to taming your legs after your motivation is higher.

It is usually better to meditate in many short sessions because one very long session will often make you tired and distracted. If as a beginner you try to meditate for a long time, you will be readily susceptible to getting drowsy. If this becomes your habit, it will then be difficult to correct your awareness so don't try to overdo it at first.

Just set a fixed period of time for a meditation session, and practice until it's over. You can even use a timer to impose discipline and regulate your sessions if you want. If you can meditate a few minutes past that amount of time, that will slowly extend your practice and pretty soon you will find an optimal amount of time that seems just right for you. It will "feel right" because you reach some degree of harmony from having adjusted your internal energy. With even more effort you will break those plateaus until you can feel balanced throughout the day.

Various Asian cultures maintain that the time you spend in meditation may initially seem like a waste of time on the surface because it doesn't seem to be producing immediate results, nevertheless meditation practice will eventually save you lots of time that would otherwise be lost in poorer health, less calm, a lower quality of life experience, and a shorter longevity in general.

9
QUESTIONS AND ANSWERS

If you really work hard at meditation practice, many questions will naturally arise. Here are answers to some of the most common questions typically asked by beginners.

Q: Do I need a special teacher, guru or "master" to learn meditation?

A: You do not need a teacher unless you want one. A special "guru" is not necessary. You don't need any type of empowerment either.

You already have all the instructions necessary to learn how to meditate in this small book. You do not need any "secret" mantra or formula or special blessing or empowerment. All you need to do is learn how to detach from thoughts to rest your mind, or learn some form of concentration to tie up wandering thoughts and produce mental peace. All the meditation practices in the world, no matter how exotic, rare or obscure, aim at helping you achieve this result of calm abiding. In practicing meditation, you are simply learning the mental skills that lead to cessation and observation, where you witness your mind, and then contemplation where you try to fathom or reason out its true nature.

If you want further details on how to practice various meditation methods, we suggest you pick up a copy of *The Little Book of Meditation* by William Bodri. This book will serve both beginners and advanced practitioners, and is one of the most comprehensive reference manuals in the world on meditation practice. This book can also serve as a teacher.

If you just want an abbreviated overview of many different meditation methods with instructions and how they work, you might want to pick up a copy of the book, *Twenty-Five Doors to Meditation*. If you want to know about all the different phenomena people experience in body and mind as they make progress with their meditation practice, you can turn to *Tao and Longevity* by Nan-Huai Chin and *The Little Book of Hercules* by William Bodri.

Q: There are so many meditation methods, so which one do I try first? Which one is right for me?

A: A person who really wants to learn meditation should try to practice several methods at the same time, but few people have the time for this. Therefore they should start by learning quiet sitting since this is the most basic and fundamental meditation technique. You sit in a meditation posture and learn how to watch the appearance and disappearance of your thoughts without attaching to them. That's the most basic form of meditation practice. You can also watch your breathing instead, and then your meditation becomes *anapana* practice rather than witnessing or contemplation practice.

The next technique you can seamlessly add to this routine without any effort is mantra recitation. Mantra recitation can be quietly performed anywhere, even at work, and fits into any time schedule without requiring any formal sitting. Therefore it is a natural add-on to any other meditation practice you choose since it doesn't require that you schedule its practice. You can mantra during any tiny bit of free time during the day, and no one will notice, so you don't have to consider this a second method but just something you would do anyway since it is so easy to fit in.

The big hurdle is not selecting which meditation method to practice, but getting someone to just sit down and meditate. Just get started, and over time you will end up trying different practice techniques. My general rule is that people should try to use a meditation method they love and one they hate, and they should also be doing mantra practice in addition to those two since you can seamlessly fit it into any type of schedule.

A meditation method you love will keep you interested in practicing meditation, but the one you hate is usually the one that will typically help you make the most progress. People usually dislike a meditation method because it is hard to do, and so that's the one that often leads to the most improvement for life in general.

People also often ask whether they should practice meditation with their eyes opened or closed. You basically use whatever is least distracting. For most people that means closing your eyes so that you are not bothered by any lights. However, some people find that keeping their eyes open helps them concentrate, so it's totally up to you as to whether to keep them open or closed.

Q: Does meditation have any religious affiliation?

A: Most religions use some form of meditation practice, but you cannot claim you are associated with a certain religion because you practice meditation. Meditation is simply a non-denominational activity used by nearly all spiritual traditions (in one form or anther), and was invented centuries ago as a vehicle to train people how to calm their minds. That is all it is. It is very natural, scientific and humanistic. There is nothing strange, mystical, mysterious, evil or devilish about it.

While used by many religions, there is actually nothing religious about it either. It is a natural skill you try to develop which leads to a peaceful mind and other great benefits. It is at the core of many self-improvement methods for "peak performance," and used to help people break harmful addictions. At its highest levels of achievement it can lead you to experiencing spiritual states, but those are non-denominational states of mind and once again, do not belong to any one religion. It is not that meditation creates new and different states of "higher consciousness," which is another big error people make. Rather, it simply purifies the mind you already have, and the degree of mental purity and clarity you attain through meditation (by eliminating wandering thoughts) is then your degree of "higher consciousness."

Q: What is the best time of day to meditate?

A: Please forget about a "best" time of day to practice. The important point is to fit meditation into your daily schedule, and that means to meditate whenever you can. Avoid doing so immediately after eating, and advanced practitioners will often find it beneficial to meditate as soon as they wake up in the morning to help harmonize all their energies.

Q: How long should a meditation session last? Is it okay if I practice for very short sessions due to the lack of time in my schedule?

A: Meditation, like most lifestyle changes, is only effective if you do it, so you need consistent practice to get results. To make real progress, it should become a vital part of your daily life. The fact that you consistently practice is far more important than when you practice, or the amount of time spent per day in meditation as long as it is a certain minimum.

We can say it is better to meditate often, for a shorter period of time, than for a longer period of time but infrequently. Furthermore, it is generally best to meditate for no less than 15 minutes per session, otherwise you are not giving yourself enough time to even get started in settling your mind. After you form a practice habit of regular meditation, you can then gradually increase the amount of time to about 20-30 minutes per session, and advanced practitioners can attempt 40-50 minute sessions if it seems comfortable.

A Harvard study found that meditating for 20 minutes twice a day was sufficient to significantly reduce the blood pressure of practitioners, but of course that amount of time would vary for everyone because of individual circumstances and considerations. Even so, this gives us a target time period of at least 20 minutes per session. An optimum amount of time dependent on this finding is to practice for 20-30 minutes with two sessions in a single day, or one session that lasts from 40-50 minutes. However, these are just general guidelines and by no means rules set in stone. Everything depends on the individual, their interest in and commitment to meditation, and their situation.

Q: My legs really hurt when meditating in a full lotus posture, so what do I do?

A: Do you absolutely need to sit in some version of the lotus posture for meditation? Absolutely not. In fact, the ancient Chinese Confucians would sit in a chair with hands on their knees, and medieval Christian monks would kneel when engaged in spiritual practices such as meditation. Many meditation sitting positions can be used; there are even positions for meditating while lying down. The important point is to get into the habit of meditation practice regardless of the posture used to do so.

You can even sit on the couch when meditating, or use other comfortable positions where the spine is erect but relaxed, but over time you'll find that the lotus position offers you the greatest benefits. Therefore we urge you to learn it. The required flexibility for assuming the position helps to open up the energy channels in your legs, and this is just one of its many benefits.

Despite being uncomfortable, it's best to try to continue holding the full lotus posture for as long as possible during each meditation session to help soften your joints, and then abandon it when it becomes too painful. Then you can assume a half lotus position or some other more comfortable sitting position. Adjusting pillows under the buttocks also helps change the pressure on your sciatic nerve when sitting, so this is often a solution that prevents the lotus position from becoming too uncomfortable. The main rule is to be at ease and thoroughly relaxed when you are meditating, and if your sitting position is preventing this, then simply adjust it.

Most devoted practitioners eventually learn the full lotus posture over time, as it helps your joints become more flexible, but it is always uncomfortable when you first start. If you do joint exercises for the knees and hips (such as Z-Health exercises), this will often help you quickly master the position.

Q: Do I have to do physical exercises before or after meditation?

A: No. However, many people will find that meditation practice ties in nicely with yoga practice and the martial arts. Actually, the *anapana* and white skeleton visualization techniques, when combined with yoga or martial arts, can help improve your skills in those areas since these meditation techniques help open up your energy channels. The soft martial arts (*Taichi*, *Bagua*, *Xing-yi*, etc.) or yoga practices can also help improve your meditation since they, in turn, help open up your body's energy channels. When practicing these exercises, you should put some special concentration emphasis on the big toes and inside of the legs running down to those toes to help open up the acupuncture meridians in the lower limbs. These acupuncture limbs in the legs are part of a full circuit in the lower portion of the body, and their opening is the key to longevity and higher meditation achievements.

Exercise helps your muscle fibers become much more differentiated and defined, and when this happens it certainly provides a better foundation for your ability to open up the *chi* channels in your body due to meditation. Only through exercise do some *chi* channels become easier to open. The martial arts, and yoga, are specially designed and therefore particularly useful to help you cultivate special postures and movements that help open up your *chi* channels and improve the *chi* flow within your body. Because it involves motion, the martial arts help for wise practitioners cultivate *chi* movements within your body that can help open up *chi* channels.

Of special help to meditation progress will be the tendon stretching exercises of *Yi Jin Jing*, joint opening exercises (such as "Z-Health"), martial arts and yoga exercises. None of these practices, if you want to master them alone, ever reach their fullest fruition without meditation. One can cultivate incredible physical skills when these physical exercises are combined with *pranayama*, internal energy work and visualization practices, but their highest levels of attainment can only be attained when they are combined with emptiness meditation.

Human beings are always seeking ways to adjust their minds and bodies in the world. Exercise, diet, sex (lovemaking skills), breathing practices, sound yoga and meditation are just a few of the methods that can help you adjust your internal energies, so it is wonderful if you learn how to use exercise in combination with these other methods to open up your *chi* channels or adjust your internal energies. This will help with your meditation practice and life in general. You can learn more about how to adjust your body in various ways through *The Little Book of Meditation.*

Q: When I meditate I sometimes get sleepy. What should I do about this?

A: If you get sleepy it's because you need to rest, so take a nap. If you try to meditate when you are extremely sleepy you are then fighting two battles instead of one because meditation requires you to stay clear in your mind, and you must fight off sleepiness at the same time. Therefore go get some sleep. Take a nap. After you are refreshed, then you can meditate. Otherwise you may fall into the habit of cultivating a dozy, unclear, sleepy state of mind when trying to meditate. You might mistakenly think this state of mind is the lessening of thoughts promised by meditation whereas it is just getting attached to drowsiness.

If you get sleepy and choose to continue meditating, you might also choose to get up and walk around, or practice breathing exercises. When you use shorter sessions it helps avoid the problem of getting tired during meditation.

Q: Are there any special vitamins or supplements you can take that will help you meditate better?

A: No. However, some people who have a yeast infection in their intestines from eating too much sugar find that when they reduce the yeast overgrowth, their mind becomes appreciably clearer and less cloudy. We want that to happen from meditation practice, but a boost in increased mental clarity often comes simply from getting rid of Candida yeast infections in the intestines. You can take a gentle nutritional product like *Candisol* to help get rid of yeast infections and reduce the toxins in the bloodstream thrown off by yeast. Those toxins tend to cloud the mind and make people irritable.

Q: Is there a special diet I should adopt to make progress in meditation?

A: Many spiritual masters recommend a vegetarian diet, or at least a diet less dependent on meat, and there are great merits and benefits to this advice. But from a practical standpoint, it all depends on your circumstances. If you were an Eskimo, for instance, this just wouldn't be possible because you would have to survive on seal blubber as a necessity. Therefore you cannot dictate dietary rules to people without taking into account their circumstances. Some people simply don't feel comfortable unless they follow a particular type of diet because the gene pool of their country has developed over hundreds of years dependent on that special diet of dairy, fish, cattle or other types of food. Their bodies may even crave a certain type of food to function well, maintain energy or feel comfortable.

Eating no meat is certainly more compassionate (and in some cases healthier) than meat consumption, and eating less meat is usually better than more, but some people don't have enough energy when they become vegetarian or cut down on their food intake. Then again, some people feel they are more aggressive due to meat consumption. What you decide to eat all depends on your circumstances, wisdom and merits. Don't let dietary rules or guidelines become an obstacle to learning how to meditate.

Q: Is meditation at all dangerous? Can it lead to possession?

A: Meditation is the practice of resting your mind of wandering thoughts. You concentrate on watching your thoughts and over time the number of random thoughts in your mind will diminish just from this detached witnessing. Your identification, entanglement, or involvement with these thoughts will diminish as well, and your mind will then become even more clear and brighter than it is now.

During meditation sessions you practice focusing on independently knowing your mind, by resting in the awareness that doesn't attach, so that you don't get caught up with errant thoughts or behaviors, but in no way does this constitute a diminution of willpower or awareness. You are actually increasing your powers of concentration, clarity and awareness through this practice of meditation. This especially makes you more resistant to negative mental states and influences, which is the exact opposite of the strange claims.

During meditation your mind remains clear, as it is right now, but it simply becomes more calm and quiet and full of less distractions. That is certainly not a form of "self-hypnosis" because you are totally conscious, clear and bright. You are not cultivating a "trance" state either where you are not aware of what is going on, and you certainly are not opening yourself up to possession.

If resting your mind is somehow evil or led to possession, then going on vacation (where you rest your mind for awhile) or going to sleep every night would also lead to possession! Clearly that is not the case. People invent all sorts of crazy notions like this in order to avoid the helpful, centuries proven practice of meditation that is recommended by countless religions and spiritual traditions. If it led to anything dangerous then countless spiritual greats would not have recommended it and religious would not promote it.

Don't ask me where these strange ideas come from. Meditation is entirely 100% beneficial. Some people even propose the idea that meditation can make you sick, too, but it doesn't make you sick either. On the contrary, meditation leads to an improvement in health, energy, balance and well-being. When your vital energy arises to contact sickness inside, it may flare up as it is being cured, but meditation energy is curing it and in no way created it.

Q: I've read that you have to be celibate to make the most progress with meditation. Is this true?

A: Not at all. Part of the origins behind this idea come from the fact that people typically lose their vital *chi* energy through sexual orgasm. Ask any man, for instance, and he will tell you he feels a loss of energy after he ejaculates semen. On the other hand, if he retains his vital energy during sex or by avoiding sex, it will remain within his body to help open up his energy meridians during meditation sessions. This is one of the reasons people have come up with this idea.

Furthermore, when someone becomes a celibate monk or

nun, the rule of celibacy is supposed to engender the disciplinary restraint that leads to the preservation and retention of these energies so that they can open up a meditator's energy meridians. Celibacy also frees you from the responsibilities inherent in a relationship so that most of one's time can be devoted to spiritual cultivation efforts instead. However, in no case does this mean you have to be celibate to make progress with meditation, or become a monk or nun to succeed in achieving the highest states of meditation progress possible.

Q: Are there any scientifically proven effects of meditation?

A: Over 1,000 scientific studies have been completed that have found countless benefits to meditation practice. Meditation has been proven, among other things, to lower blood pressure, increase blood circulation, reduce serum cortisol (the stress hormone), lower the frequency of hospitalizations, reduce chronic pain, improve one's ability to relax and deal with stress, reduce reaction times, reduce the problem of insomnia, reduce blood sugar levels for diabetics, improve memory, increase attention spans, sharpen focus, improve self-control, reduce cases of depression, help break addictions, improve work habits, increase regions of the brain cortex dealing with memory and decision making, and slow aging. With all these benefits, what's not to like about it?

BOOKS OF INTEREST

If you are interested in more details about meditation for health or spiritual cultivation, you might be interested in articles on the website www.MeditationExpert.com and these other publications that deal with more detailed aspects of meditation practice:

Twenty-Five Doors to Meditation, William Bodri & Lee Shu-Mei.

The Little Book of Meditation, William Bodri.

The Little Book of Hercules, William Bodri.

Internal Martial Arts Nei-gong, William Bodri & John Newtson.

Tao and Longevity, by Nan Huai-Chin & Chu Wen-Kuang.

Spiritual Paths and Their Meditation Techniques, Nan Huai-Chin & William Bodri.